Y0-ACA-453

No Further Retreat

ALSO BY RAYMOND F. DASMANN

The Destruction of California
A Different Kind of Country
The Last Horizon
African Game Ranching
Environmental Conservation
Wildlife Biology

NO FURTHER RETREAT

The Fight to Save Florida

RAYMOND F. DASMANN

Drawings by ELIZABETH DASMANN

The Macmillan Company, New York, New York

Collier-Macmillan Limited, London

COPYRIGHT © 1971 BY RAYMOND F. DASMANN

All rights reserved. No part of this book may be
reproduced or transmitted in any form or by any
means, electronic or mechanical, including
photocopying, recording or by any information
storage and retrieval system, without permission in
writing from the Publisher.

The Macmillan Company
866 Third Avenue, New York, N.Y. 10022
Collier-Macmillan Canada Ltd., Toronto, Ontario

Library of Congress Catalog Card Number: 79-143780

FIRST PRINTING

Printed in the United States of America

Contents

Maps

Foreword

FLORIDA IS ON the edge of the tropics. This has been a major influence on its history, a source of its present conflicts, and will be a determinant of its future. It is the reason for this book, since I have long been intrigued by the tropics, finding them a fascinating area for ecological inquiry.

This book had its start in 1967; I had hoped that it could be finished quickly and become a useful tool for those who were working to save the Florida environment. Unfortunately, I could not go on quietly doing studies for my book while the environment that I was writing about was being destroyed. Again and again it was necessary to put aside the writing in order to join in a conference, meeting, or some other activity conducted by my Florida friends in their efforts to protect what was rare or wild or beautiful. Furthermore, I have been painfully aware of the inadequacy of my own knowledge. No person can know an entire state, or even a Florida county.

My original editor, Peter Ritner, who encouraged me to start on this effort, was patient and forebearing, but time went by and it was necessary for him to leave in order to take a more exalted position elsewhere. His successor, Howard Sandum, perhaps reconciled from the start to the absence of any visible manuscript, let me keep to my slow pace. Nevertheless, since I do not want to write a history of a state that no longer exists, I am bringing this book to a conclusion. It does not tell *all* about Florida. My emphasis is clearly on the southern part of the state, and there is much that I have yet to learn even about this region. I cannot pretend that this book will be up to date by the time that it appears in print. In Florida, change comes too quickly. Nevertheless I write with the hope that some ideas presented here will prove useful to those who are working to keep Florida a fit place for people, and that this effort may help enlist some new recruits for its cause.

RAYMOND F. DASMANN

Morges, Switzerland

Acknowledgments

THIS BOOK IS a cooperative effort, even though my wife and I must take the blame for the contents. From the time we first started to work in Florida, we have received help and hospitality at every hand. It is difficult to begin to acknowledge and thank all those who have assisted us. Florida has an unusual and highly dedicated group of people who are working in an effective way to save their state. Few states have people who are both willing and able to work together with a minimum of conflict and controversy in an area that unfortunately is too commonly beset with internal rivalry.

For our knowledge of the Florida Keys, we are particularly grateful to Sandy Sprunt of the National Audubon Society, Jack Watson of the Bureau of Sport Fisheries and Wildlife, and Frank Craighead, Sr., of Homestead, Florida.

Frank Craighead has been our principal guide to the Everglades region, but we have also been helped by Bill Robertson, Roger Allin, and Jack Raftery of the National

Park Service, and Robert Padrick, former chairman of the Central and Southern Florida Flood Control District.

In the Naples area, Joel Kuperberg, Bill Vines, Jack Allen, Nelson Sanford, and many others have been helpful and hospitable to a degree that we cannot begin to repay.

For information about Florida in general we are particularly grateful to Nathaniel Reed, now Assistant Secretary of the Interior and a man who has done more to change the political climate in Florida to favor conservation than has any other single person. We cannot begin to thank Lyman Rogers, at that time chairman of the Governor's Natural Resources Committee, for his willingness to drop whatever he was doing to guide us around central Florida. We owe a great deal to the Partingtons, Bill and Joan, of the Florida Audubon Society; to Marjorie Carr of the Florida Defenders of the Environment; to George Cornwell of the University of Florida; to Durbin Tabb and Bernie Yokel of the University of Miami; to Ross Allen, Buck Ray, and their colleagues at Silver Springs. Art Marshall, now of the University of Miami, has been a major guide into the ramifications of Florida's estuarine ecology.

This list could go on for pages and still not cover all who have assisted in gathering material for this book or who have offered hospitality. We have been flown in planes and transported by boats, cars, and air boats over much of Florida by them. We have been fed, housed, entertained, and informed. We are deeply grateful.

In particular, however, our debt is to Russell Train, past president, and Sydney Howe, president, of the Conservation Foundation, who made it possible for us to spend time in Florida and provided financial assistance for our Florida travels.

Palm Hammock

Introduction

THERE ARE PLACES on earth where nature has blended its aspects of sea and sky, land and life, in ways that appeal most strongly to the human spirit. Florida is one of these. Here the basic theme is the meeting of land and water, to be elaborated on land through luxuriant tropical or subtropical woodlands adorned with a diversity of vividly colored birds, and in the water by an even greater luxuriance and variety of aquatic life. It was inevitable that people would gather on the Florida shore and that their numbers would increase. It was inevitable, also, that their aspirations, expressed in ways adapted to more simple and sturdy landscapes, would come into conflict with the natural rules that governed the functioning of the complex and fragile Florida terrain. When such conflict occurs, there is usually time for men to consider their actions and seek new ways for living within the natural rules. In Florida, there is still time. Failure to achieve a new solution can only lead to the destruction of all those things that made Florida worthwhile. Success can enrich life for all.

In the past man has too often destroyed the beautiful places and blasted the productivity of the lands and waters on which his survival depended. We can readily see his record where the remains of ancient cities in devastated landscapes bear witness to dreams that have vanished and hopes that failed. But in the past the efforts of mankind were localized, and always beyond the boundaries of the human estate were other places where nature could survive and ultimately repair the damage. Today, humanity is widespread, with power and influence beyond earlier imagining. No place is entirely spared. No place is secure. Failure to adjust to environmental reality brings the risk of a broad, more universal collapse.

Florida today has all the environmental problems that beset the technologically advanced nations of the world. It has its ugly, confining urban ghettos and its suburbs that march in endless, monotonous ranks, where people are boxed like expendable commodities in uniform containers. It has been spared, thanks to its weather, from the worst ravages of air pollution, but its waters are becoming as foul as any. Perhaps the Miami River and the St. Johns cannot match the Rhine, the Tiber, or the Hudson for sheer filth, but they are serious contenders. Tampa Bay can rival Lake Erie or the Baltic Sea in the race to extinction. These are the problems that exercise the minds of people and governments in the "environmental decade." But Florida has other problems, and in these areas it is a leading contender

Florida is on the edge of the tropics.

for first place in the nation's chamber of environmental horrors. These involve the destruction of all that is priceless and rare, unique and irreplaceable, in an environment of unparalleled value.

It is unfortunate that the great wave of concern for the human environment has centered so strongly upon the urban-industrial scene and its problems of congestion and pollution. Nobody can deny the importance of these aspects, but they are perhaps too obvious. No city exists by itself. Each depends upon the broader array of farm and field, forest and mountain, for its survival, and these are being battered by forces that may have their origin in the cities, but exercise their effects far from the metropolis. In Florida, the conflict between technological society and the irreplaceable values of the natural landscape is most severe.

3

Introduction

If pollution is the most serious problem in the great metropolitan centers, then lack of control over land-use is the most serious problem in the total world environment. In Florida, this lack of control has been most clearly exemplified. In Florida, the means for control must now be found.

The people of Florida have been given trusteeship over the only continental area of tropical life within the United States. They control the future of a heritage of plant and animal richness that cannot be matched elsewhere. Florida is no ordinary state to be handled in the usual, careless way. To maintain the intricate and fragile balance between terrain and life in Florida requires greater skill and perception on the part of its custodians than is required of people in less-favored lands.

The 1970s opened with a great concern for the human environment. Despite the fickleness of the communications media, this concern for the environment will not fade away. The problems are real. If they get worse, many will suffer and many will die, and the demand for action will take a violent turn. If the efforts to solve these problems are successful, people will be encouraged to persist and to achieve more and more. Either way—in a peaceful progression or in the excesses of outrage and despair—the environmental movement will remain active.

The environmental crusade of 1970 with its Earth Day, its ecology weeks, and its environmental action programs led to many oversimplifications of the truth and to an equal number of untruths. But the principal message came through—man cannot survive if he ignores the state of his environment. He is tied, along with all other living things, by the network of ecological relationships within the

4

biosphere—that thin film of earth, air, water, and life on the surface of the planet. If this network is too seriously disrupted, all will perish together. This message came through in a forceful way, but the other side of the story did not receive its share of attention. Life is tough and resilient. The creatures that have inherited the earth have survived ice ages and arid heat, hurricanes and floods, fire and earthquakes and volcanic outpourings. They can be pushed to the wall, but given half a chance they spring back. The forces of destruction that man has let loose on the planet, while drastic, are seldom new. Man did not invent pollution. He was not the first to create barren, lifeless surfaces on the planet. He did not invent radioactivity, violent explosions, or destructive force. Admittedly he has accentuated all these to a point of potential catastrophe, but given any sensible degree of control over his future behavior, the forces of nature will repair and correct his past mistakes. Environmentalists have preached a sermon of impending doom. It is necessary also to proclaim the message of hope. Only with hope comes the willingness to work, to fight for improvement—the determination to build on earth that kind of world in which free men can thrive. Today it is urgent that we have the hope, the willingness, the determination, to work and fight for a better world. There is no time for defeatism or despair.

In the pages that follow, the nature of the lands and the waters of Florida will be explored, and some of the rules that govern their operation will be examined. In Florida, we will see that there are delicate, natural balances that are readily disturbed by human activity, but there is also a resilience that permits recovery. Florida has been badly damaged. Were the damage irreparable, there would be no point in calling for action to save the environment. But it is not irreparable, at least not yet. In a land of fire and flood, tossed by hurricanes and battered by the sea, life develops resurgent powers. These provide the means through which man can work toward a better future.

Ways out of a complex environmental dilemma are never easy to find or to follow. There are three forces operating in Florida, and over the world, which in combination create the serious problems of the environment that now confront us. Population growth is one of these, but as we will see in Florida, control of such growth alone could at best provide for some alleviation of environmental problems. The absence of control over the employment of modern technology is the second major force which leads to unexpected or unplanned-for outfalls in the form of pollution or the disruption of ecological networks. But control over technology alone will not answer Florida's problems. The lack of control over land-use, already noted here, is a third, obvious, and severe cause of environmental disruption. But land-use control alone will not solve Florida's environmental difficulties. An integrated approach to all these forces is required, but most particularly a kind of leadership is needed that has not previously been available, a leadership that will assume responsibility for the total environment.

Much has been lost in Florida, but a richness remains. As one looks out, for example, through a screen of palms, sea grape, and casuarina at the beach of Naples and the wild Gulf beyond, it is difficult not to become a Florida booster. But the knowledge is there that Florida boosting and the consequent uncontrolled and unplanned spread of people and their technologies have been the curse of this state.

As one looks out at the beach at Naples and the wild gulf beyond . . .

If Floridians grow more conscious of the importance of the *irreplaceables* in their land—the wild things and unique landscapes—if they take time to shape the growth and development of their state, to control it so that it enhances rather than destroys nature, then a bright future lies ahead. Florida is in a unique position to set an example, not only for the United States, but for the West Indian region to which it also belongs, a region in which island governments grapple with the same problems that beset Florida, but with fewer resources to apply to their control. If Florida fails, it will pioneer the way to complete environmental collapse in other places as well.

No state is under greater pressure from all the forces that place demands upon land, water, and life. But in no other state are the environmental issues so clear, the natural values so high and so obvious, the ecological rules so easy to understand, and the consequences of failure so disastrous. Few other states have the combination of a political leadership that is growing more enlightened and a citizenry

7

growing more dedicated to the environmental cause. The opportunity to win exists in Florida. The consequences of failure are unacceptable.

The United States begins or ends in Florida. There is no further retreat than its tropical shores and islands. If we do not win the battle for the human environment in Florida, we will probably not win it anywhere. This is the challenge that Floridians must face.

Gulf Storm

1 : The Tropical Borderland

THERE ARE MANY ways to occupy yourself if you have
nothing urgent to do, and one of these is weather watching.
In Florida the habit grows on you easily. Since the land is
flat, the sky fills more than its usual share of your field of
vision. Clouds provide the verticals in a landscape where
horizontals dominate.

On the Gulf coast of Florida, if you happen to occupy a
place near the beach, the summer sky over the Gulf of
Mexico can become a major feature of each day. It is seldom dull. The day may start bright and clear, but it rarely
ends that way. Sunsets are uncommonly dramatic with
blazing reds and yellows following through the spectrum to
greens and cool violets. Usually there is a massive thunder-
head herding a flock of clouds slowly across the horizon.

9

Lightning will pound down at a ferocious rate, with some of the bolts of unbelievable size and fury—yards wide, pouring a steady stream of electricity into the sea. Rarely, a truly massive storm will trail dark waterspouts behind it, sucking up moisture from the Gulf and hurling it heavenward, only to pour it down once more in a driving tropical rain. Should one of these waterspouts reach the land, it achieves the more formidable title of tornado. Despite what the Florida boosters say, tornadoes are not infrequent in this land of the hurricane, but compared to the damage done by a tropical hurricane, the tornado's effort seems somewhat minor and localized.

I have been in swimming when one of Florida's summer thunderstorms has started to approach, and like all others, I have left the water. I wondered what happened to fish and other sea creatures when that massive voltage from the heavens jolted the seas, but I prefer to ask an authority rather than experience it for myself.

Despite what you may read, the environment in Florida is not mild. Winter, when most northerners come to southern Florida, is the quiet season, likely to be marred only by a stretch of northern weather, that has lost itself in journeying across the continent, bringing rain and cold too far south. These cool spells can, and sometimes do, last all the way through an outlander's two-week vacation and send him home to Poughkeepsie or Pierre feeling betrayed and disillusioned. But during most of the year, it is the warm mugginess of the weather and the slashing storms that impress the visitor.

Since a warm, humid environment is one that favors all those creatures that lack an internal temperature-regulating device, the Florida environment favors the so-called cold-blooded creatures. It is a land where reptiles and amphibians thrive, but more than that it is a land of insects. Any idea you may have of wandering through the Florida wilds clad in shorts or a bikini had best be forgotten, or you had better stay on the wider beaches. Away from the seashore, where only the sand flies will bother you, is the realm of the mosquito. Florida's mosquitoes may not be the world's largest or fiercest, but you will not notice the difference. On the Gulf coast, in the mangrove country, they reach an unusual level of density and hunger. Folk tales tell of people stranded in the Everglades' mangroves who were found dead and drained of blood the next day. When mosquitoes fill the air around you and evening is approaching, you may find yourself believing that these stories are true.

Mosquitoes have ruined more wilderness experiences than the wilderness buffs will ever admit. They bite through clothes with no difficulty, and I am almost prepared to say that some of them bite through boots. Mosquito repellent is better than nothing, but in some areas I think that the mosquitoes have learned to love it. A mosquito net would keep them away, but it would also cause its wearer to expire from the heat. Alcohol is said to help, by some. You feel less pain.

Mosquitoes are such a major factor in the Florida environment that all lesser problems, such as those offered by cotton mouths, rattlesnakes, copperheads, coral snakes, and the great array of other biting and stinging creatures, seem inconsequential by comparison. They have caused the National Park Service to bow to circumstances and use insecticidal sprays and dusts in such areas of human concentration as Flamingo. This helps a bit. Most of the major towns and cities include mosquito control as an essential budget item. Even the most ardent follower of Rachel Carson is forced to compromise.

But all these environmental problems are familiar to those who know the tropics. The tropics are noted for having an array of those forces that add up to "nature in the raw." They are violent climes, for the most part, and the gods of tropical peoples are not known for benevolence. Shiva, the destroyer, of the Hindu trinity, and Hurakán of the Caribbean Indians, whose wrath is expressed in the tropical storm, come to mind.

There is an imaginary line around the earth called the Tropic of Cancer. It passes just to the north of the Hawaiian Islands and Cuba, cuts through the Sahara and the Arabian Desert, bisects India and Taiwan, and carries on across the Pacific. To the traditional geographer, this marks the northern boundary of the tropics; just as far to the south the parallel Tropic of Capricorn marks the southern boundary. The Tropic of Cancer is the line on the earth's surface on which the sun appears to rise and set on the longest day of the northern year, June 21. This is the most northerly advance of the sun during the northern summer, 23½ degrees north of the equator, just as Capricorn is the line of the most southerly advance of the sun during the northern winter. These tropic lines have, therefore, great significance, but the forces that move air and water around the surface of the earth, and through these determine the climates of the earth, do not pay great respect to such boundary lines. Since climates determine to a great degree the kinds of plants and animals that can live on the earth, it follows that the earth's biota is also not greatly influenced by the lines marking the northernmost or southernmost positions of the sun. The climatic and biological tropics therefore are not defined by Cancer or Capricorn.

Ecologists have long recognized the tropical nature of southern Florida. C. Hart Merriam, who classified the climatic and biotic regions of North America into Life Zones, recognized southern Florida as tropical. Frederick Clements, who is responsible for the classification of North American vegetation into climax formations, puts southern Florida into a tropical formation. Finch and Trewartha, in their geography of North America, place southern Florida in a tropical climatic region. Any biologist who has worked in the tropics will feel at home in the hammocks, the mangrove swamps, and the palm groves of southern Florida. It is clearly tropical. Northern Florida, on the other hand, along with the Gulf Coast from Alabama to Texas and the coast north to the Carolinas, is subtropical, according to any reasonable biological classification.

Yet, tropical Florida is cut off from the main area of distribution of tropical species. From their long-established centers in the equatorial regions of Amazonia in Brazil, tropical species extend northward, with few barriers, through northern South America and up through Central America into Mexico. Northward from Venezuela, however, their distribution is hindered by oceanic gaps. Trinidad, close to the South American mainland, and connected to it in the not-too-distant past, shows close relationships biologically with the flora and fauna of mainland America. Farther north, however, Dominica shows marked differences from the forest flora and fauna of the mainlands. The species that have reached Dominica, a volcanic, oceanic island, have been those adapted to crossing water barriers by one means of transportation or another. Cuba and the Bahamas are still farther away, and show even greater impoverishment in the numbers of tropical species represented on their shores. Southern Florida is the northern-

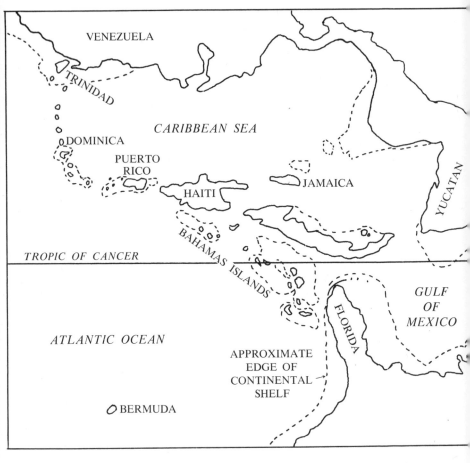

Florida and the West Indies.

most extension of the tropical West Indian flora and fauna. From a biological point of view, it is an island cut off from the main centers of tropical evolution and from the areas where tropical species are in their greatest concentration. Like an oceanic island in tropical seas, it could be reached only by those species that could be carried by storm winds or rafted on the Gulf Stream to its shores.

Florida is therefore a tropical borderland, a bridge between the tropics and the subtropical and temperate zones farther north—a northern outpost of the West Indian region. It is an area where we can study the interplay and interaction between the biotas of the temperate continental region to which it is connected by land and the more climatically similar island regions from which it is separated by a water gap.

CLIMATE

Each winter the storm tracks of the north are followed by the whirling cyclones and anticyclones of North America. From their regular beat leading from Washington to Maine, they dip southward in varying degrees, pouring down snow, sleet, and hail upon most of the temperate zone. As temperatures dip to freezing, and to subzero levels in the northern United States, the northerner can watch with interest as the temperature readings from southern Florida come in on the daily weather report. Sooner or later it will dawn on him that down there things are different. But most people who could afford to notice such things noticed them a long time ago. The coasts of southern Florida are ringed with winter refugees from the north.

The popular image of the tropics among those who dwell in temperate lands is usually based upon conditions that exist in the humid lowland tropics, where temperatures are uniformly warm and rain falls throughout the year. This is the region that supports the great tropical rainforests of Brazil, the Congo, and southeastern Asia. But included within the tropics are high mountains and deserts, places high enough to be covered by perpetual snow and areas where rain may never fall. Perhaps the largest area within the tropics is one where temperatures and rainfall show a seasonal variation, that has one or two dry seasons per year alternating with one or two rainy seasons. During the dry seasons, it is common for temperatures to be lower than they are in the wet seasons. Such areas support a dry forest vegetation, in which the trees are usually deciduous, shedding their leaves in the dry season, regrowing them in the wet. Often these forests have been opened up by fire or other influences into extensive savannas, areas in which grassland alternates with woody vegetation or in which trees are dotted over a grassy terrain.

Tropical borderlands generally have both wet and dry seasons; it is into this climatic type that both tropical and subtropical Florida fit. Winter in Florida is drier and cooler than summer. In subtropical Florida, temperatures may drop to freezing on some occasions, and the battle to save the citrus crop from frost will begin. In tropical Florida, it will become too cool for comfort during these cold periods. Occasionally, some rain will fall in winter, but this is uncommon in the tropical belt. Summer, however, is a wet period, with most rain falling from convectional storms with their dramatic displays of lightning and crashing thunder. Humidities are high, and away from the immediate sea coasts where winds bring some relief, the climate is uncomfortable for most people.

Autumn in Florida is hurricane season. In this, Florida and the West Indies share the plight of the similar tropical borderland of the East Indies and southeast Asia. Generated in the equatorial oceanic regions, these whirling, low-pressure areas usually move along a clockwise path in the

Northern Hemisphere, from the Atlantic across to the West Indies, northward through Florida and then up the Atlantic coast, commonly moving offshore as they swing north until they are dissipated in the North Atlantic. But hurricanes are peculiar, erratic storms that cannot as yet be forecast nor their courses predicted. They may depart from their normal path to veer westward across the Gulf, striking at Texas and Mexico. They may reverse their path and move back southward when all have relaxed in the belief that danger has passed. They may, as Hurricane Gladys did in 1968, stop for a time off the Florida shore and then suddenly cut in at right angles to hit where they are not expected.

Real estate salesmen and developers, and all others who seek to bring people to Florida, prefer not to talk about hurricanes. But hurricanes come to Florida every year. There are bad years and good years, but at any time from summer through fall you can expect a hurricane. If you are lucky, it will not hit where you are. If you had foresight in choosing the location of your house and constructed it well, you may weather a hurricane when it does hit. The people who live on volcanoes, who build homes on an earthquake fault, or who dwell on a flood plain are not necessarily fatalists. They may be only poorly informed. Recent arrivals in Florida are particularly easily deceived into thinking the hurricane will not come. But, sooner or later, it will come.

A hurricane is, to speak in mild, unemotional terms, a howling monster of a storm. It is not possible to say how strong the winds become because during the worst ones the anemometers have broken. A weather bureau observer who lived through the September, 1935, hurricane on

17

Long Key estimated velocities up to two hundred miles per hour, and such have since been recorded.

The 1935 hurricane of the Florida Keys was for many years the best known and best documented of the ferocious hurricanes of Florida. It took place before the present hurricane warning system was instituted, roaring north from Cuba to smash without warning the central Keys. The observer on Long Key, J. E. Duane, first noted trouble at 2:00 P.M. on the afternoon of September 2. The barometer had started its rapid descent to what was to be a record low of 26.35 inches. Heavy seas and high tides along with rain squalls were observed. Rain continued, and with it high seas, until 5:00 P.M. when hurricane-force winds first hit and the rains increased.

The force of the winds continued to build. By 6:45 P.M., heavy timbers were flying. A 6-inch by 8-inch beam, 18 feet long, was blown through Duane's house. By 9:00 P.M., all the houses were being wrecked by flying timbers, including the main lodge to which Duane had moved. Then, more than four hours later, at 9:20 P.M., the storm abated, the sky cleared, wind and rain ceased.

The calm eye of the hurricane passed overhead for nearly an hour. During this time, however, the sea continued to rise, floating the last standing building from its foundations. At 10:15 P.M., hurricane-force winds returned, blowing from the southwest instead of the north as before. They wrecked the last remaining house and blew Duane into the sea. Somehow he managed to grab a coconut tree before being knocked unconscious. Some hours later he came to and found himself 20 feet up, clinging to the tree. By 5:00 A.M., the hurricane-force winds and high seas abated, and it was safe to move around once again.

Less fortunate than Duane was a crew employed by the Federal Emergency Relief Administration for work on the Keys as part of the government effort to solve the unemployment crisis of the thirties. When news of the coming hurricane reached Miami, a train set out to rescue these workers. It was blown off the tracks. At least 190 of the FERA workers were lost in the storm. In addition, 170 or more residents of the central Keys were killed or lost. When the final tally was in, it was believed that some 400 lives had been taken. The towns of Tavernier, Islamorada, and Marathon were hardest hit. The center of the storm cut a swath of nearly complete destruction 30 miles wide.

In all hurricanes that hit the Florida coast, damage by water equals or exceeds damage done by wind. The 1935 storm was accompanied by seas reported to be 18 to 20 feet high. This was unusual, but seas up to 8 feet above mean high tide are not uncommon. At Naples in 1960, Hurricane Donna brought tides of 6 feet or more, but houses with foundations 8 feet above mean high tide escaped water damage. On the Keys, hurricane-wise builders use reinforced concrete pillars to raise houses 8 feet above the ground. But the reckless or gullible still build or buy seaside houses built at ground level.

The incredible destruction wreaked by Hurricane Camille in Mississippi in August, 1969, virtually wiping out Gulfport and Biloxi, makes one realize that no structure can be entirely secure. Although publicized as the worst hurricane in history, it is doubtful that Camille could hold up against some of its predecessors. These hit less heavily populated areas, but they took far more lives.

In September, 1926, a hurricane moving in from the Bahamas crunched down on Miami and Fort Lauderdale.

The old mangroves were smashed and battered by the force of the hurricane.

Thousands of buildings were destroyed and many lives were lost. Hitting Lake Okeechobee, this hurricane blew the water over the dikes built at the southern end of the lake to protect the agricultural lands. In the town of Moorehaven and its vicinity, the lake waters took 320 lives. Only two years later, in 1928, another hurricane smashed in from the Atlantic at West Palm Beach and once more hit a Lake Okeechobee that had been filled by the preceding rains. Water poured again over the farming towns and agricultural lands. When the final toll was known, 1,800 people had been lost. From these two storms the drive to control the waters of Okeechobee and the Everglades had its beginning. The army engineers moved into the Everglades. They have never left.

Hurricanes have helped to build Florida. The tropical

species of plants and animals that inhabit the southern peninsula have come, in part, on the storm winds from the south, often finding a home in new land created where hurricanes have piled up mud, shells, and debris. But, in payment for any gifts they may bring, the storms do as much damage to the wildlife and wild landscapes as they do to man-made structures. As a result of Hurricane Donna, which swept over the Everglades in 1960, and Hurricane Betsy, in 1965, tens of thousands of acres of mangrove forest were killed. The magnificent forest of the Shark River country, perhaps the oldest and tallest mangroves on earth at that time, was smashed and battered. Admittedly the mangroves are growing back, but it will take a long time with freedom from hurricanes for them to recover their previous grandeur. Another instance of this is the ancient oak groves along the Mississippi coast which were destroyed by Hurricane Camille. Although mangroves and live oaks are not endangered species, there are plants or animals that have dwindled to small numbers because of man's activities. One hurricane's hitting a small population in a restricted habitat could mean the end of the species. Even though man scars more landscapes and endangers more species than were ever harmed by hurricanes, it is the combination of the two, the senseless forces of unplanned human activity and the random violence of hurricanes, that offers a new threat to the Florida environment.

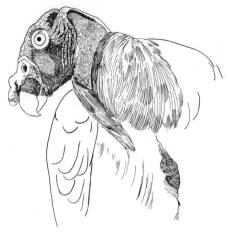

King Vulture

2 : *Land and Life*

LAND

FOUR THOUSAND FEET below the surface of the ground at Ocala in the north-central hilly region of Florida lies the core rock of the Floridian plateau. This is a southward extension of the rocks that underlie the Piedmont region of the southeastern United States, a mixture of igneous and metamorphic rocks such as one would find exposed in the southern Appalachians. Long ago, these basement rocks were eroded and warped downward to be covered by the sea. They are the foundation on which Florida has been built—a peninsula of submerged rock that rises from the deeps of the Gulf of Mexico on the west and falls off steeply into the depths of the Straits of Florida on the east. This foundation is much wider than the present state of Florida. The edge on the west is a hundred miles offshore from Sarasota. Out to that distance the water is shallow, gradually deepening to 300 feet at the edge of the plateau. Beyond that it falls off rapidly to depths of 12,000 feet. On the east the land lies close to the edge of the plateau, and just offshore from Miami, the continental edge falls off to depths of over 2,000 feet, rising again sharply to the Bahama banks, approximately fifty miles east of Miami.

All peninsular Florida that stands above water—the state of Florida that exists today—has been built on this basement rock, primarily by the action of living creatures. To a degree unique in the United States, Florida is of biological origin. It is also a state whose future survival will depend on the care that is taken of the living creatures that live on it or surround its outer rim.

In southern Florida, no well has yet been drilled deep enough to locate the basement core of the state. At Sunniland in Collier County, where Florida's only active oil field is located, a well 12,000 feet deep is still being drilled through limestone. This limestone was formed in calcium-rich seas that covered the old Floridian plateau repeatedly during past geologic ages. Calcium carbonate was drawn from the water by the action of marine organisms that formed it into their shells and skeletons. Upon their deaths the shells were deposited on the floor of the sea to be compressed gradually and consolidated into limestone rock. Elsewhere, carbon dioxide released by the respiration of marine organisms caused calcium carbonate to be precipitated into small nodules that grew and grouped into masses shaped like fish-egg clusters. Of such a nature is the Miami oolite that underlies the Everglades and most of the eastern part of Florida and the lower Keys. Other areas were built up by the action of coral polyps, drawing calcium carbonate and other minerals from marine waters to form their stony coverings, turning eventually into coral rock. In yet other places, countless shells of marine organisms were washed up by the tide and storms to form bars, and in time, islands of shell sand, such as Sanibel and Captiva off the Gulf coast. Wherever mangroves grow, they are building land, and where they have grown for long, a tough layer of mangrove peat is left behind as a semipermanent contribution to the land mass of Florida. Where land has been formed and the vegetation of dry land or fresh water invades, its mass increases from year to year, and the litter and debris it leaves behind decays and crumbles to form deep organic soils, thus building higher the surface of the land.

The Florida of today can be understood only when viewed against the past. The deep foundation of the state has been one of the most geologically stable areas on earth. The layers of limestone have not been twisted or folded, but only warped upward to a height of around one hundred fifty feet near Ocala. The Ocala limestone dips down on a slope of about five feet per mile, and away from Ocala is covered by more recent limestone deposits. At the tip of Florida, the top of the Ocala formation is 1,200 feet below the level of the sea. This limestone was deposited far back in the Eocene age, when the ancestors of today's mammals had wrested control of the earth's dry land from the giant reptiles of the past. But only sharks and fishes then swam over what were to be the plains of Florida. Succeeding epochs of time, the Oligocene and the Miocene, saw further layers of limestone deposited in the Florida Sea, formations that were to be known as Suwannee Limestone, Tampa Limestone, and the Hawthorn

Formation, where sand and clay washed from a land mass in what was to become northern and western Florida were added to the foundations of the Florida peninsula. When the Pliocene epoch arrived, perhaps twenty million years ago, the shape of Florida began to appear above the sea. Land life invaded where only sea creatures had lived before.

The record of vertebrate fossils from Florida tells the story of peninsular formation. During the long Age of Reptiles, the Mesozoic, land life was well developed in the American West, but there was no Florida. The only fossil from a Florida formation of this age, brought up from a 9,210-foot well-core near Lake Okeechobee, is that of a marine turtle. During the Eocene, the first epoch of the Age of Mammals, the Cenozoic era, the dawn horse roamed the Wyoming plains. But in Florida there are only fossils of extinct whalelike creatures that cruised in an ancient sea. Following the Eocene, the Oligocene epoch in Florida produced fossils that indicate the presence of only seas and fishes. In the succeeding Miocene, the central epoch of the Age of Mammals, Florida first began to emerge as dry land. Only the north-central and western regions reveal mammal fossils. We know that at this time, the three-toed horse, a large bearlike creature, and some ancestral coyotes, badgers, skunks, camels, and deer were wandering about in this area. Most of the peninsula remained a place where limestone was deposited and marine creatures held sway.

There are relatively few fossil locations from the next, Pliocene, epoch, but these suggest an abundance of large mammals in Florida. Mastodons and mammoths, rhinoceros, horses, camels, and antelope roamed the land. The final, Pleistocene, epoch, when ice sheets covered the north and sea levels were low, found Florida teeming with land life. The array of mammals of all kinds—elephants, mastodons, and giant sloths to bats, moles, shrews, and rodents—was enormous. Mixed in with the bones of extinct species have been found the bones of primitive man, who at some time during these glacial ages reached Florida. Since man has arrived on the scene, the other mammals have been leaving it. The pattern of extinctions has brought the disappearance from Florida of ground sloths, giant armadillos, giant beavers, capybaras, wolves, spectacled bears, jaguars, saber-toothed "tigers," mastodons, mammoths, tapirs, horses, peccaries, camels, bison, and elk.

The Pleistocene in Florida was a period of ups and downs. There were four major glacial ages which, starting from the most recent, are known in the United States as the Wisconsin, Illinoian, Kansan, and Nebraskan. During these, the seas withdrew from the Floridian plateau since much of the water of today's oceans was tied up in continental ice sheets. But during the intervening, interglacial stages, sea levels rose. Thus, during the stage following the Nebraskan ice age, the sea may have stood at two hundred seventy feet, high enough to cover peninsular Florida. Following the Kansan ice age, the oceans rose once more and reached a probable level of two hundred fifteen feet above present sea level. In the Sangamon interglacial, before the most recent (and perhaps continuing) Wisconsin ice age, sea level appears not to have been so high, but was at least twenty-five feet above present levels, high enough to cover most of southern Florida. Much of what is now the Everglades and its coastal adjuncts has probably emerged from the sea in relatively recent times. During the past five thousand years, however, sea levels in Florida have again been rising. The remains of flooded forests lie beneath the waters of Florida Bay and the Gulf of Mexico.

WILD LIFE

At the time when the thirteen colonies to the north were seething with revolution and a spirit of independence, William Bartram was beginning his travels in a Florida that had only ten years before become staunchly British. He went alone into what was then mostly an unknown wilderness, up the St. Johns and the Oklawaha rivers into the Ocala country, to describe the strange clear springs that bubbled up from limestone caverns and to see plants and animals that were not then known to the European world. His travels took him through the woods and savannas of Florida's central highlands, and then on to the Suwannee and across to the established settlements of West Florida. His remarkably accurate journal provides our first view of the primitive wilderness of Florida, a view which reveals major differences from today both in the abundance and variety of wild creatures.

Traveling up the St. Johns River, Bartram was beset by alligators. These were not the small and wary creatures of today, but large—up to 20 feet long—and unquestionably aggressive beasts. They surrounded his boat and threatened to climb in, forcing him to retreat to shore. On shore he spent a miserable night, trying to keep his campfire burning brightly enough to repel the advances of the giant reptiles. Even allowing for a certain distortion in his writing caused by his panic, we must accept his record of both the size and aggressiveness of these wilderness gators. None that survive today would trouble Bartram in such a way. Farther along in his travels, Bartram went through a full-fledged Florida hurricane. His account of that occurrence leaves little doubt about his ability to report accurately during times of stress and danger.

Bartram often saw wolves in the Florida of those days, obviously common and not much bothered by the sight of man. These Florida wolves were a black, melanistic phase of the species *Canis niger,* now surviving only as the endangered red wolf of the Arkansas–Texas region. In Florida, they were to disappear during the nineteenth century. The last record of one is from the Miami region in 1854.

At Manatee Springs on the east side of the Suwannee near Chiefland, there were still manatees in Bartram's day. Today the species still holds out in small numbers in the Suwannee and Crystal rivers and farther on to the south.

Perhaps one of the strangest accounts, however, is of a vulture which Bartram observed in addition to the usual turkey vultures. His detailed description of this large bird leaves no doubt that it was the king vulture, a species which survives today only in South America and which has not been seen in Florida since Bartram's day. We cannot blame man for its disappearance. Perhaps, a breeding population came northward, pushed by the forces of a storm, settled for a time, but could not adapt to the changing environment of this tropical border region. Most likely there have been periods of more severe climate in Florida since Bartram's time than there were in a long period preceding his visit. He describes royal palms up to ninety feet in height

Royal palms still survive in
tropical Florida.

growing north of Lake George. Today they survive in a
wild state in a few places in tropical Florida far to the
south. Francis Harper, who edited Bartram's journals, pos-
tulates that the severe freeze of 1835 may have finished off
this northern outpost of the species. Certainly the severe
winter freeze of 1970 did serious damage to garden palm
trees and other planted tropical species in the same region.

An early indication of the exotic invaders, both plant
and animal, that were to plague Florida in the years to
come is provided by Bartram's account of the wild oranges
that he found growing widely throughout central Florida.
These were the Spanish bittersweet oranges brought to the
early missions and Spanish settlements. From there perhaps

they were carried by the Timucua Indians on their journeys inland, and the seeds were dropped at their campsites. Birds may have spread the seeds further. Obviously these oranges were well able to adapt to their new environment and compete with its native plants. Bartram found them growing in woods and hammocks, inland and beside streams, forming in places extensive wild groves.

Apart from these more unusual observations, Bartram encountered the trees and flowers, the birds and wild mammals that are still to be found in Florida today. The difference then lay in the abundance and in the more fearless behavior of animals in the presence of man.

Bartram's enthusiasm for Florida was unabated. He wrote of wandering in a wilderness Eden, in a world we have now left far behind. But most of the wild things that he saw are still with us, and we still have wild places. With some minimum display of foresight and common decency we can keep them into the future. It is, after all, the vegetation and animal life even more than the climate and topography that make Florida different and a place worth living in. It is vegetation and animal life, also, that hold Florida together, keep it above the sea, make it function, and enable man and all his works of concrete and plastic to survive.

The dynamic pageant of life has gone on through the ages in Florida, building and shaping the land that has become the state. Downward from Georgia and Alabama have moved the trees, herbs, and grasses of subtropical and temperate America. Upward from the Indies have come the tropical invaders. In Florida they have met and interacted, forming different kinds of communities, finding new ways for previously separate species to live together. The climate, the nature of the soil, and the level of water have set the stage for life, but these too have been dynamic and ever changing. When a warm cycle of weather has prevailed, tropical forms moved north, displacing their temperate-zone rivals; when cold fronts swept southward, they were forced back. Much of southern Florida, only newly emerged from sea or swamp, is scarcely stabilized, providing fair ground for competition between the older species of Florida life and the new arrivals carried by currents, storms, or man.

Northern Florida has little to distinguish it from the rest of the southeast. Here are the same savannas of longleaf pine and hardwood forests of oak and hickory mixed with amounts of pine varying in accordance with their history of fire and the character of their soils. Perhaps these forests are more laden with Spanish moss than their counterparts farther north, but they are little different in most other respects. A more Floridian character appears in the piny flatwoods where an overstory of slash pine shades a shrub layer of saw palmetto over many a monotonous mile. In their primeval state, these were fascinating forests, but few areas are more dull (to anyone but a timber grower) than a managed, second-growth forest with trees of one age class predominating. Too much that one sees today is in this condition.

Towards the coast, differences begin to appear. There is a region along the Apalachicola River west of Tallahassee that rates the characterization of unique. Here was a thriving stand of a conifer related to the yew, the stinking cedar (*Torreya taxifolia*). This belongs to a genus whose only other species, the California nutmeg, occurs in the wild Santa Lucia mountains of California. Some unknown blight has hit the Florida species, and it appears to be dying out in a wild state. In the same region, however, is the true Florida yew (*Taxus floridana*), another species restricted to this area. Also here is found the corkwood tree (*Leitneria*), another rare plant, along with the sand hickory and cherrybark oak. These join with other species of wider distribution to form an unusually rich tree flora. It is said that in a single day's walk around this area, one can encounter a hundred species of trees along with a much greater number of associated shrubs and herbs. Such diversity is common enough in the tropics, but rarely encountered this far north. Fortunately, part of this region is protected in the Apalachicola National Forest.

The vegetation along the larger streams in northern and central Florida has a tropical aspect. Here grow the tall, buttressed bald cypresses that produce for aeration of their roots the cypress knees that are featured in Florida curio shops. These cypresses are one of our few deciduous needle-bearing trees. In winter they stand in a leafless state, looking dead among the surrounding evergreens, but ready to sprout new leaves and new growth when spring arrives. Joining with the cypresses in the riverine woodlands are cabbage palms, sweet gums and black gums, magnolias, water oaks and laurel oaks. All are commonly bearded with that aerial relative of the pineapple plant, the Spanish moss, which hangs in gray festoons from even such sterile sites as telephone wires.

The shoreline vegetation, and that of the offshore islands, is sufficiently distinctive to deserve special attention. Perhaps the most varied development is to be found on St.

The bald cypress in its leafless state looks dead among the surrounding evergreens.

Vincent's Island, recently acquired as part of the national wildlife refuge system. Since I will describe this in some detail later, I will not attempt to do so here.

The central Florida highlands that extend as far south as Fisheating Creek, draining into Lake Okeechobee, are not highlands in any usual sense, since their elevation rarely exceeds two hundred feet. However, they represent land that has been above the sea for relatively long periods of geologic time, and which is Florida's closest approach to hill country. The aspect is indeed hilly. When I first visited this region, driving through on the highway, it was a cool and rainy day. In the mist it was easy, if one did not look closely, to imagine oneself in western Britain. The illusion was created by the well-kept pastures and woodlands, the rolling country, and the glossy livestock. But a close look would dispel the illusion. The woods are subtropical, with magnolia and evergreen oak, cabbage palm and sweet gum. Here, too, are extensive areas of upland pine forest, and east of Ocala, in an area known as the pine scrub, is a region where sand pine, scrub oak, and saw palmetto grow in the deep sandy soils of an ancient Pleistocene dune land.

From the Suwannee south along the coast on the west and from Cape Canaveral on the east, the shoreline becomes increasingly tropical. Mangroves begin to dominate the river mouths and estuaries; beaches are backed by palms and the introduced casuarinas, or Australian pines, of tropical Pacific shores, along with the colorful sea grape. Inland the piny flatwoods, or grasslands with cabbage palm islands, give way in the south to the great Everglades' "river of grass" or to the extensive cypress swamps of the Big Cypress country. In the south also appear the tropical hammocks, small forests of enormous vegetational diversity, and the more tropical Caribbean pine forests of the Everglades region. Northern species of plants begin to fade from the picture and tropical trees, shrubs, and herbs—species unknown elsewhere in the United States—dominate the scene. This is the land of strangler fig and gumbolimbo, of mahogany and the poisonous manchineels, of coconut and thatch palm, and an impressive list of plants known best to those who have studied tropical vegetation.

Although the vegetation of Florida is sufficient to make the average ecologist or botanist from the north run in small circles giving out cries of pleasure, it is the animal life, and in particular the bird life, that attracts most visitors. The tourist may grow disgusted with mangroves and bored with piny woods, but few seem to complain of a surfeit of spoon-bills or a plethora of wood storks.

Florida's mammals differ little from those of the south in general, but Florida has become what may be a rapidly vanishing refuge for species that have become extinct farther north. The Florida panther is the same puma, cougar, or mountain lion that was once abundant throughout the United States. In the West this big cat still holds on in fair numbers, but the eastern form of the species has vanished except for the Florida population which belongs to a separate race from the former, more northern populations. In Florida, the panther very nearly followed the wolf into extinction, but its more solitary and secretive nature—it does not run in packs nor howl to advertise its presence—per-

Home of the strangler fig and a great diversity of tropical forest trees.

Panther

mits it to hold on in the wilds of the Everglades, the Big Cypress Swamp, and a few other wild regions. Somebody has guessed that there may still be one hundred panthers in Florida—but we know only that some survive since they are seen occasionally. Nobody has yet devised a way for counting panthers.

The principal prey of the panther is the deer, and in Florida, this remains one of the most abundant large mammals. Florida deer are of four races. The widespread

Virginia white-tailed deer (*Odocoileus virginianus virginianus*) enters Florida from the north and extends down the central highlands. On the west the coastal regions are inhabited by the Florida coastal white-tailed deer (*O. v. osceola*), and on the east and south, by the Florida white-tailed deer (*O. v. seminolus*). The outer Florida Keys support the distinctive pygmy race of white tails, the Florida key deer (*O. v. clavium*). Except for the key deer, it is difficult to distinguish one race from another. The situation has been further confused by man's introduction of other deer from Texas, Wisconsin, and North Carolina into Florida and by the shifting of native deer from one part of the state to another. This was all done with the best of intentions and under the illusion that such introductions would increase the numbers of deer and preserve better health and conditions among the hybrid stock. It has, however, interfered with the opportunity to study how the native populations adapted to their differing kinds of environment. Even the Keys have not been left alone, since some well-intentioned person has introduced the northern white tail to previously deerfree Lignum Vitae Key, where they are now overly abundant.

One of the strange mammals of Florida is the manatee. This animal belongs to a sea-going order of mammals, the *Sirenia,* named after the sirens or mermaids that sailors used to see before scientists told them that they couldn't. To placate the sailors, scientists have assured them that what they had been seeing were not beautiful women with tails like fish, but ugly old sea cows—one of the least beautiful mammals. The sirenians are divided into two families. One contains the dugongs of the tropical Indian Ocean, southeast Asia, and Australia (now nearing extinction) and the Steller's sea cow, which once inhabited the Bering Sea until it was wiped out by Russian fur traders, Aleuts, and their associates, who wished to eat it and make skin boats from its hide. The other family contains the manatees. There are three species of these. One, now nearly extinct, occupies the Amazon River drainage of South America. The second, probably also greatly endangered, lives in the rivers of West Africa. The third, Florida manatee, once ranged into the rivers and estuaries all around the rim of the Caribbean and through the West Indies.

Manatees are completely harmless creatures and might even be considered friendly, although this could be the result of either poor eyesight or sheer stupidity. They are enormously useful mammals since they have a great appetite for the water weeds with which the waterways of Florida are becoming choked. Nevertheless, they are hunted illegally by the casual vandal with a rifle or by those who want a taste of the meat. In the United States, the Florida race has become extinct all along the Gulf coast from Texas eastward and on the Atlantic coast north of Florida. In Florida, it persists only in a few areas. The status of manatees in the West Indies is uncertain, and it is likely that the Florida population, depleted though it may be, is the best hope of the species for survival.

Among the commonly observed mammals of Florida are the armadillos or, more strictly speaking, dead armadillos since they are common highway casualties. However, this mammal does not belong in Florida at all, being normally a denizen of the Southwest and Mexico. Some years ago, it was liberated in Florida, thrived in its new environment, and is now widely distributed. The species is the nine-banded armadillo, a member of a family that occurs for the most part in Latin America. With its leathery hide and tendency to curl up into a ball when threatened, it is a most unlikely looking member of the order of mammals.

Florida's reptiles include the creature that has received major publicity in the 1960s, the alligator. This species once ranged abundantly throughout the American Southeast and, as Bartram noted, was a formidable animal in the days before man was equipped with modern firearms. Now alligators have been greatly reduced in numbers, mostly because alligator shoes and handbags are popular fashion items among women, but also because the demand for water has resulted in the destruction of much former alligator habitat and because the tendency to fill in swamps and marshes to create new residential sites has destroyed even more. The alligator is a fresh-water reptile, although it does range into the brackish water of estuaries.

There are only two species of alligator on earth: one in China, if it still survives; the other in the American South. It is difficult to love alligators. They are neither beautiful nor friendly, in fact to most people they appear ugly, treacherous, vicious, and stupid. But their role in maintaining the environment on which hundreds of other wild creatures depend is significant. In the Florida environment, the alligator is important in much the way that the elephant is important to African wildlife. Alligator holes in the swamps, kept open by their rubbing, digging, and scraping, often provide the only water in which fish and other aquatic creatures can survive the dry seasons, and further provide drinking places for many wild animals.

Most people confuse alligators and crocodiles, but the two are not very closely related. In Florida the crocodile is easily distinguished by its long narrow snout, compared with the blunt nose of the gator, and by its preference for salt or estuarine water, compared with the fresh-water preference of the alligator. (By the way, the baby gators still sold, live or stuffed, in Florida, are neither alligators nor crocodiles, but caimans, a South American species.)

In early days crocodiles ranged up the Florida coast as far north as Lake Worth. Now they are restricted to the tip of Florida and the Keys and are close to extinction in the United States, although they survive in Central America and the West Indies. It is even more difficult to grow sentimental about crocodiles than about alligators, since they appear less beautiful to most people and less reliable in their behavior towards man. Yet they too play their role in the great web of life that acts to keep planet earth alive and functioning and a fit place for that most unreliable of animals known as man.

One of the most famous members of Florida's crocodile clan was Old Zulu, whose stuffed skin may still be viewed at Ross Allen's Reptile Institute at Silver Springs. He was shot at Biscayne Bay in 1922 by a member of a survey party. Thinking him dead, a surveyor went over to kick the crocodile, but found too late that he was still alive and able to administer a fatal wound. In the confusion that followed the unfortunate incident, a local opportunist captured the crocodile and kept him alive until he had recovered from his wounds, when he was sold to the Reptile Institute. At Silver Springs he lived for 30 years and grew to a length of 15 feet. In 1952, he made the mistake of threatening an alligator, Old George, of larger size and weight, who finished him off before the two could be separated.

The other large reptiles of Florida are sea-going members of the turtle tribe. Virtually all these are to some degree in danger of extinction. The green turtle, the ridley, the leatherback, the loggerhead, and the hawksbill turtle all occur in Florida waters, and some of them used to nest in good numbers on Florida's beaches. However, human pressure on these beaches has virtually destroyed their usefulness as turtle nesting grounds. The big animals are now restricted to the more remote and protected areas. The big loggerheads still heave themselves up on the beaches of Jupiter Island, Captiva, St. Vincent, and a few other places to lay their eggs in the late spring or early summer. On Cape Sable in Everglades National Park, in addition to encouraging the loggerhead turtles, an effort has been made to establish a population of green turtles, brought from their home beaches in Costa Rica by Professor Archie Carr of the University of Florida, and his students. This species has been greatly depleted by human predation for its meat, for the calipee inside the shell, which is its contribution to turtle soup, and for the shell itself. The largest of the sea turtles, the leatherback, may reach a length of eight feet in shell length. Most of the others seldom exceed three feet. A close rival in size to the sea turtles is the alligator snapping turtle which inhabits the fresh waters of the Suwannee drainage. These may reach a weight of well over one hundred pounds.

Florida's ichthyologists and herpetologists point with pride to the fact that the lands and fresh waters of Florida contain more species of reptiles, amphibians, and freshwater fish than any other area of equal size in the world. There are 333 kinds listed by Archie Carr and Coleman Goin in their book on this subject, including one species each of alligator and crocodile, 35 kinds of turtles, 25 lizards, 60 snakes, 29 salamanders, and 28 frogs. Fishes which occur in fresh water, 154 species, bring the list to its peak. Salt-water species of fish are even more numerous, many hundreds of kinds, and oddly enough a great number of these come up the fresh-water streams to lie about, for reasons of their own, in the crystal waters of Florida's famous limestone springs. At Silver Springs, Homosassa, and elsewhere, one may watch great numbers of marine fishes —snook, snappers, sea trout, and others—mixed in with the fresh-water forms.

Tourists usually are impressed by the various kinds of poisonous snakes that are to be found in Florida. There are three kinds of rattlesnakes, including the big, tough old diamondbacks and canebrake rattlesnakes. There is a copperhead, a cotton mouth, and two races of coral snake. All these can deliver a poisonous bite, and Florida can give rise to as many hair-raising tales of snakebite or near snakebite as any place in the United States. Still, the chances of having a dangerous encounter with a poisonous snake are really quite remote for most people and not in any way to be compared with the risks that they run in daily life on city streets and on the highways from encounters with their fellow human beings.

Florida's fish, however, are of much greater interest to both Floridians and visitors than are Florida's snakes. The varieties of sport fishing that are still available in Florida are enormous, ranging from the quiet cane-pole fishing for catfish in some Everglades canal to searching out the wily snook in a Gulf coast estuary to fighting raging battles with marlin or sailfish in the Gulf Stream. Commercial fishing in Florida is equally important; among the finned fish, mullet, snapper, sea trout, pompano, mackerel, menhaden, and grouper are the leaders in value. However, shrimp, crab, lobster, and the various mollusks far exceed fish in their commercial worth to Florida fishermen.

I will not attempt to enlarge on the subject of fisheries at this point, but must point out how impressed I have been by Florida's sharks. Flying just offshore down the length of the southern Atlantic coast, I have counted hundreds of sharks cruising lazily out beyond the breaker line of beaches where great numbers of people were basking or swimming. If my view of the scene could have been reflected down to those who were so happily pursuing sea-shore sports, there would have been a rapid and massive exodus from the water. Perhaps, ignorance can be bliss, since I am told that Florida's sharks rarely bother people. I don't really believe this, however, when I am in deep water. Even small barracuda bother me.

Florida's birds rate high among its tourist attractions. These vary from the usual southern-state species of northern Florida to the exotic tropical forms of the Everglades and the Keys. In the dry season of late winter, when water birds are concentrated along the permanent streams and ponds, the variety and abundance of bird life seem truly spectacular. Yet what may be seen today is only a fraction of the abundance of a few decades ago. There are many reasons for this: the pressure upon water resources, the filling in of marshes, and the "reclaiming" of land from estuaries which reduces the amount of habitat suited to water birds each year. But of all the factors threatening Florida's bird life, none has been more insidious than those related to the continued use of the persistent "hard" pesticides of the DDT–dieldrin group. Despite efforts to restrict their use, they are still sprayed and dusted by farmers who seek a cheap and easy way around their insect pest problems. And so we cannot say how much longer the bald eagles and ospreys, the brown pelicans and white ibises, the roseate spoonbills and reddish egrets will continue to breed or thrive in Florida. We know they are all in danger.

Seminole Village

3 : History and People

NOT ONLY IS Florida different geologically and biologically from the rest of the United States, it has also a markedly different history. It is linked more closely to Cuba than to New England.

It is impossible to know which European vessel and which white man first saw the shores of Florida. The Spanish were in and around the West Indies starting with the arrival of Columbus in 1492. As they destroyed and exterminated the native peoples and cultures of the West Indies, they went farther afield in search of Indian labor to work the mines and plantations. Quite probably the first Spanish visitor crashed his ship on the coral reefs of the Florida Keys and was seen no more. But before anyone from Spain officially reached Florida, an English ship from Bristol, captained by the Venetian John Cabot, sailed down its coast in 1497 and recorded the nature and extent of the land and the abundance of its fisheries.

To keep the earlier historians happy, credit for the discovery of Florida is usually given to Juan Ponce de León, who came north from Puerto Rico in 1513. In legend, he was searching for the mythical Fountain of Youth. In fact, he did not consider himself old and was, instead, looking for wealth and power along with his contemporaries. He hoped to stake his claim in the Bahamas. Somewhere on some unknown Atlantic beach in central Florida, Ponce de León and his men carried the red and gold banner of Spain to shore and claimed the land for their monarch. They left us no useful description of what they saw. Farther south, perhaps on Jupiter Island, the Spanish discoverers had their first brush with Florida's Indians and a foretaste of things to come. Accustomed to the peaceful Arawaks of the Indies, the Europeans were not prepared for all-out war. But Florida's Indians had been forewarned by their Caribbean brethren and were not about to become willing victims or peaceful serfs. The Spanish ships put out to sea once more and followed along the coast and the line of the Keys to the Dry Tortugas.

Every effort that the Spanish made towards settlement and colonization of Florida was resisted violently by the Indians. Piñeda traveled off the Gulf coast in 1519. In 1521, Ponce de León returned to the vicinity of Charlotte Harbor, where he received a fatal wound from the Calusa Indians that brought his Florida ventures to an end. Narvaez landed, presumably at Tampa Bay, in 1528 and marched north to Apalachee Bay. De Soto landed at some controversial point, perhaps on Tampa Bay, in 1539 and went by land up the coast past Pensacola. The first actual settlement, at Pensacola, was established 20 years after De Soto's landing, by Tristan de Luna y Arellaño, but this was abandoned two years later. Other attempts at settlement were also ill-fated, and Spain might have forgotten Florida (as it would have forgotten California) had other nations not taken an interest in using it as a base to intercept the Spanish treasure ships bearing northward from the Spanish Main on their way to Europe.

When René de Laudonnière came out from France in 1564 to establish Fort Caroline, north of what is now St. Augustine, the die was cast. The next year Pedro Menendez de Aviles set forth from Cádiz with a great fleet to drive

Florida Place Names.

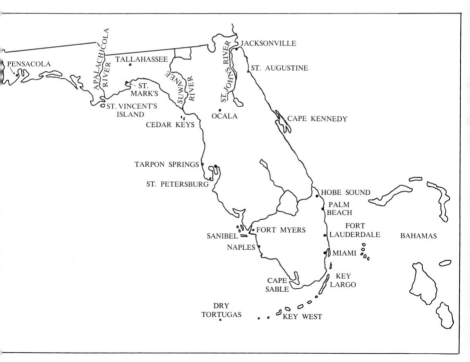

the French from Florida and establish, once and for all, the hegemony of Spain. He succeeded admirably in both missions, and in 1565, St. Augustine came into being. Thereafter the Spanish remained, gradually extending a chain of missions and forts across northern Florida. It is worth noting that St. Augustine was established 22 years before the first English attempt at colonization of Virginia, the ill-fated Roanoke Colony of Sir Walter Raleigh, and 42 years before Jamestown was colonized by Captain John Smith and his companions in 1607.

Although the Spanish established their claim to northern Florida, creating a barrier to the southward movement of the English and French, southern Florida was to remain Indian country. Despite numerous efforts, it was neither conquered nor colonized. It was to become, however, a refuge for various runaways and renegades, for former slaves and grounded buccaneers, who mixed and mingled with the Indians with varying degrees of acceptance. In the north the Spanish missions succeeded where arms had failed in gaining the friendship of the Timucuas and other tribes. A friendly feeling toward Spain slowly developed, even in the south. But the earlier hatred for the Spanish was transferred to the English, who in the seventeenth century were raiding the Florida coast to pick up slaves for their West Indian holdings. Marjorie Stoneman Douglas notes that when Jonathan Dickinson was shipwrecked on the coast, near the mouth of the Loxahatchee, in 1696, the Indians knew only one English phrase, which was "English son of a bitch."

Unfortunately, Florida's Indians were to fade away, not from conquest and defeat, but from the effect of European diseases—smallpox, measles, and all the other ailments to which the white men had built up resistance over long centuries of exposure, but against which the Indians had no resistance. We do not even know what they looked like. Their old cultures are forgotten; their times of greatness have faded from memory. The survivors, here and there, were to mingle with the Indians who were to replace them and, like them, go undefeated in the wilds of southern Florida—the Seminoles.

Seminole is a word said to be derived from the Muskogee Indian language meaning "people of the distant fires." In its Florida usage, it came to mean those Indians who came to the peninsula during the eighteenth century and gradually pushed southward to escape the pressure of the white men. Included were the Muskogee-speaking tribes, generally called Creeks by the English, who had come from west of the Mississippi and occupied the Gulf and southern Atlantic coastal country. Included also were the Hitchiti-speaking peoples of the same coastal region, of whom the Mikasukis were to become the best known.

At the time when Florida was ceded from Spain to Great Britain in exchange for Havana (which the British had captured during the Seven Years' War), it had a mixed population. In the south were the remnants of the Calusas, Tekestas, Matecumbes, and other Florida Indians, along with miscellaneous refugees. In the center and north were various tribes to be known as Seminoles, along with villages of escaped Negro slaves, the Maroons or Cimarrons, who lived as free men in peace with the Indians. The Spanish settlements were chiefly at St. Augustine and at St. Marks. The British were vigorous colonists and, with their West Indian experience, were able to establish thriving plantations along the northern Florida coast. But they did not remain for long. With the American Revolution lost and trouble brewing once more in Europe, they swapped Florida back to Spain in exchange for the fortress of Gibraltar and the islands of the Bahamas in 1783. For the next 35 years, Florida was to remain under tenuous Spanish control. The English, French, and Americans contested ownership of its western corridor. Creek Indians fleeing from the whites, and runaway slaves drifted across its borders.

The existence of Florida as free territory located right on the border of Georgia and Alabama was a thorn in the side of the slave-holding states of the American South. Upon their insistence, the United States purchased Florida from Spain for $5 million. The purchase served largely to legalize a conquest that had already occurred. General Andrew Jackson, leading the Tennessee militia, and entirely on his own initiative, had captured St. Marks and defeated a mixed force of Seminoles and Maroons. Before Florida became a state, he was already seeking to crush the remaining Indian forces on the Suwannee River. The Seminoles, under a leader called Bowlegs, were heading south for the Everglades. Spanish authority had already vanished when Andrew Jackson arrived. He was to remain as territorial governor of Florida—an enemy of the Indian and a strong believer in slavery.

Despite Jackson and all who were to follow him, southern Florida remained a refuge for all who could flee there. The Seminoles produced remarkable war chiefs, Osceola, for example, and Chekika—who knew all the hammocks and hiding places in the Big Cypress and the Everglades— Billy Bow Legs, and Tiger Tail. Their names remain on the land and are claimed by their descendants and by many who are not descendants at all. The Seminole Wars dragged on. The white soldiers also performed remarkable feats of exploration and wilderness survival in their endless pursuit of the elusive Indians. Nobody really won the war. Eventually treaties were signed that were no longer broken by either side.

As a consequence of its history, Florida played a mixed role in the Civil War. Nominally it was a Southern slave state and part of the Confederacy, but it contained many who sided with the Union. The wilderness regions and the Everglades coast became a refuge for draft dodgers from both sides, along with the still-undefeated Seminoles. Key West went for the Union, becoming a base for the naval blockade against the South. Near present-day Miami, Fort

The Big Cypress Swamp and the Everglades were a sanctuary for refugees from the north and the Florida Indians.

Dallas remained a Union post. The Union held Fort Pickens at Pensacola and easily captured Fort Myers. Out on the Dry Tortugas, Fort Jefferson was built to serve as a prison for captured Confederate soldiers. There may have been 150,000 people living in Florida during the war days, and for most of them, the war was somewhere else. Slavery vanished from Florida in 1865, but except for the plantation country in the north, its passing was scarcely noticed.

From its different beginnings, Florida went on to develop differently from the other states of the South. In some ways it became two separate states: agricultural Florida with its strongest base in the north, but including other inland rural counties; and urban Florida, centering on Miami and the other major cities, but occupying all the more easily developed sites along the coast. The former is closely allied to the rest of the South, but with its own flavor—inclined to support conservative Democrats, and voting heavily for George Wallace in the 1968 elections. The latter is more closely allied to the industrial North and to the Middle West and inclined to support liberal Republicanism. Until reapportionment, following the Supreme Court decision of 1964, control of Florida politics tended to rest with the agricultural counties. Since then, it has shifted to the urban areas, but the rural interests are still strong. Its state government is organized in such a way as to be barely functional. The governor has little authority since his so-called cabinet is made up of independently elected members who are often at odds with him. The cabinet does exercise real power, but has tended to reflect "pork barrel" interests. A strong governor can exert some leadership through his direct influence with the people; but, being conspicuous, he also must take the blame for actions that are carried out by the cabinet against his wishes.

Florida differs from most other Southern states also in the relative percentage of Negroes in the population—only 20 percent in 1960. The black people are largely centered in the agricultural north and the irrigation-agriculture area around Lake Okeechobee. Their percentage in the population has declined steadily from nearly 50 percent at the end of the Civil War, when most of Florida's people lived in the northern part of the state. Despite a much higher birth rate among Negroes, this percentage has continued to decline because of the strong tendency to migrate to Northern industrial cities.

Florida's rural population is predominantly Florida-born and often made up of people with a long family history in the state. It includes therefore many who feel strongly about their Floridian heritage and are highly concerned with protecting the quality of the Florida environment. It also includes, unfortunately, many who hope only to make a killing from the sale of their land to the first developer who comes along and then to get as far away as possible from the natural environment. The urban population includes a high percentage of newcomers to Florida—people who came south to retire, to establish a second home for winter use, or to work in sophisticated modern industries, such as those associated with the space-age complex centered at Cape Kennedy. Unfortunately, many of these think of their true home as New England, or Minnesota, and not as Florida. Their interest in Florida, outside of their own backyard, is minimal. In the 1960 census, it was found that only 37 percent of Florida's people were native born —the other 63 percent had come from other states or other

Once a last outpost in the Florida wilderness, Smallwood's Store at Chokoloskee still looks out at the wild Ten Thousand Islands.

countries. Among the latter, many have come as refugees from Castro's Cuba, and they still come. Miami has been their principal area of settlement, and the Cuban colony there has given a cultural diversity to the city that had previously been lacking.

It can be argued that the chances of meeting a Floridian in Florida are rather small. In addition to the permanent immigrants, Florida attracts tourists who outnumber the natives by a ratio of more than 2 to 1. In 1960, with 5 million people residing in Florida, 13 million tourists visited the state. In 1970, 20 million tourists were expected. In 1960, tourists spent some $2 billion in Florida and were the state's largest source of income. The factors that attract tourists to Florida—scenery, climate, beaches, fishing, boating, outdoor sports, and its historical heritage—are obviously of prime importance to the economic future of the state. Tourists put unusual pressure upon the state's outdoor resources, but provide a major argument for maintaining the Florida environment as something different, for shaping development to enhance the unique qualities of the state, and for preserving that quality of tropical or subtropical nature that provides the needed contrast with the man-made world.

The rate of population growth in Florida, although encouraging to boosters and speculators, is frightening to those who prefer not to see one continuous complex of Miamis, Fort Lauderdales, and Tampas covering all the state. In the 50 years from 1850 to 1900, the population increased sixfold. This increase, however, took place in a near-empty state, so that by 1900, only 530,000 people lived in Florida. By the early 1950s, the population had again increased sixfold, to over 3 million people. In the succeeding 15 years, it doubled again, and in 1969, exceeded 6 million inhabitants. These were not distributed evenly around the state, but were concentrated in the more favorable coastal areas, particularly the Miami–Palm Beach region and the Tampa–Fort Myers strip. In 1960, 74 percent of the people were urban or suburban, and only 2.3 percent actually lived on farms. Although 6 million people are not many by New York or California standards, they exert enormous pressure upon the limited supply of land suitable for residential development and upon the state's fragile living resources. The hope of attracting still more millions leads the road builders, the jetport builders, and the residential developers to take points of view that

55

have not been favorable to maintaining the quality of the Florida environment.

Many who came to Florida saw the state as a retreat, a refuge from the pressures associated with life in their former hometowns, a place to take life more calmly, to enjoy the sun and the out-of-doors. But now the pressures have followed them, as their numbers have grown, and the availability of the out-of-doors diminishes each day. Viewing the unique Florida environment, its wildlife and fisheries, its vegetation, shorelines, islands, and waterways, Florida's people are developing a growing realization of its total irreplaceability. Recognizing that there can be no further retreat, that they must protect what they have, they have begun to make a stand.

Anhinga

4 : Rookery Bay

HALFWAY BETWEEN Naples and Marco Island is Rookery
Bay. In this part of Florida, in the past, Rookery Bay did
not differ markedly from a dozen other bays and estuaries.
Until quite recently, it did not even support the bird
rookery from which it presumably was named. Yet Rookery Bay has achieved a status out of proportion to its assets.
It has become both a battleground in the new struggle for
Florida and, perhaps, a model to show how future battles
could be avoided. It is a place where new tactics and new
strategies have seemed to offer hope for the future of the
Florida environment.

Although Rookery Bay is not unusual within its region,
the region is one of compelling natural beauty, not to be
duplicated elsewhere in the United States. Stretching from

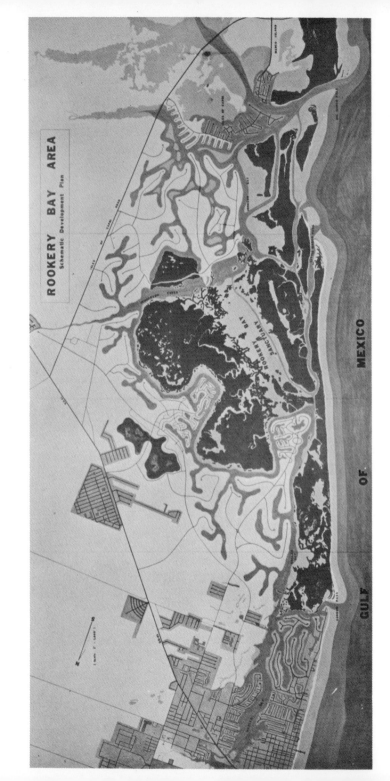

ROOKERY BAY AREA
Schematic Development Plan

Naples southward through the Ten Thousand Islands to Cape Sable, it was one of America's last frontiers, and is still largely wild. It is a wilderness more of water than of land—of mangrove swamp and sandy key—where flocks of water birds of outrageous shapes and startling colors still find a home and where one of the continent's richest fisheries finds a basis for its support. It is a sanctuary for some of America's rarest animal and plant life. Perhaps most of all, it is a challenge to the American people.

Here the American passion for growth and development encounters the reality of America's irreplaceable natural resources. To be resolved is the question of whether or not growth can be controlled and channeled in a rational and orderly manner so that the environment that first attracted such growth is not destroyed. To be decided is whether it is possible to develop a region in which people may live without ruining those features that have made them want to come there. To be examined is whether it is possible for Americans to live in a place of beauty without making it ugly.

Rookery Bay, Naples, and Marco Island are located in Collier County, rated as one of the most rapidly growing counties in the United States. Naples, although still only a moderately sized town, has become a center for regional growth that has spread rapidly to the north and east, and has now begun to move southward along the edges of the Gulf, through the mangrove-lined channels, bays, and estuaries that feed into its marine waters. The land to the southward, and in particular the water, has always been a part of the Naples environment, valued by its residents and tourists alike for its wild qualities and its special kind of fishing in waters remote from population pressure—fishing shared with raccoons and ospreys, eagles and egrets, but so far not with too many of the human species.

The threat to this environment did not begin in earnest until the decision was made to develop Marco Island, the largest, most unusual, most biologically unique island of the Ten Thousand Islands region. This decision, made in the early 1960s, created a new center for population growth less than ten air miles south of Naples. It led to speculation on the development values of all the lands in between, including those surrounding Rookery Bay. Some looked with anticipation to the profits to be realized if a continuous city were to spread from Naples to Marco and on into the Ten Thousand Islands wilderness. Others were appalled by this prospect, recognizing that the environment that had attracted them to this part of Florida would be destroyed. In 1964, the two groups came into conflict when a proposal to build a road into the Rookery Bay area, and thus open it to real-estate development, was presented to the Collier County commissioners.

In Florida, those who favor real-estate development have been accustomed to winning their battles. The state and all its constituencies have favored growth, as representing progress, and have done everything to encourage it. Conservation groups have protested, but such groups have been weak, disorganized, and politically ineffective. One who would like to pick up the flavor of such early conflicts can find it best presented, fictionally, in a novel by John MacDonald entitled *A Flash of Green*. MacDonald, author of such stories of crime, sex, and sudden death as in his well-known Travis McGee series, has in this book described the struggle and ultimate defeat of the "Save Our Bay" group in a town that seems remarkably like Naples.

A wilderness more of water than of land.

Marco Island before development—the largest, most unusual, most biologically unique island.

But in the real Naples, things may be tending towards a different ending.

Naples is inhabited, fortunately, by numbers of people who, appalled by the strip-city development of Florida's east coast, sought to create in their part of Florida a city that differed in all ways from Miami Beach. The prospect of being submerged in a randomly developed hodgepodge Gulf metropolis appealed to them not at all. The prospect of losing the wild land and water that they still considered as their backyard appealed even less. Organizing themselves into a group called the Collier County Conservancy, those who were interested in preserving Rookery Bay won their first battle. The proposal to build a road into the Rookery Bay region was defeated.

It was apparent to the conservancy, however, that winning a battle to stop a road was not enough. So long as the lands surrounding Rookery Bay were privately owned, the threat of development would remain. The conservancy therefore organized a drive to purchase sufficient land to provide for a major sanctuary of undeveloped open land, islands, and channels around the bay, which could stand as a barrier of wild country between any development that might spread up from Marco Island or down from Naples. The value of the bay as a fish and wildlife sanctuary was explored and verified by marine scientists from the University of Miami and by other biologists. Public support for the project proved to be forthcoming. Donations, large and small, came in from throughout the community.

Recognizing that the conservancy could not expect to patrol and manage the sanctuary after it had been purchased, it made an agreement with the Audubon Society, through which the society would participate in the purchase and serve as trustee of the lands after their acquisition. By the end of 1967, the local conservancy, working with the national Nature Conservancy of Washington, had raised the $450,000 needed to acquire 2,600 acres of land, privately owned, that surrounded the 1,500 acres of state-owned submerged land in Rookery Bay. The Rookery Bay Sanctuary, of 4,100 acres, under the management of the Audubon Society, came into being. A permanent warden, Jack Allen, was assigned to the job of protecting it.

Thus far the struggle had followed the lines of a traditional conservation effort, although it was distinguished by success. On one side were those who favored development; on the other were those who wanted preservation of nature. Feelings ran high and words were acrimonious. But there was a difference. The conservancy enjoyed a remarkable degree of community support, and the community was remarkably wealthy. There was an unusual degree of talent and energy to be found in Naples, willing to be put to work for the cause of the environment. The leadership of the conservancy rested initially in the hands of Charles Draper, who had a considerable amount of wealth and great capability for organization. Later, after his death, it passed to the equally capable hands of Nelson Sanford and Willard Merrihue. But all who were concerned agree that much of the drive of the organization centered in its executive secretary, Joel Kuperberg, a botanist who was then the manager of the Caribbean Gardens and who served as a member of the Naples City Council, but who nevertheless found time to spearhead the conservancy effort. Much of the professional talent in the Naples region was enlisted in one way or another into the conservancy cause. Such names as Lester Norris, of the Texaco Oil Company, and Julius

Fleischman were to be found among those who provided financial or other support. The Collier Company, founded by Barron Collier who once had bought the entire county from a willing state government, took a favorable view of the conservancy effort. Furthermore, and this may be the most significant difference from most conservation–development battles, the conservancy did not stop working after the land had been purchased and the sanctuary established. They had learned in the course of the struggle that in Florida buying a sanctuary and setting it aside is never enough.

To understand the Rookery Bay problem, it is necessary to look at the environment of southwestern Florida and the ways in which human activity have affected it. Southern Florida is a meeting place of land and water. The ways in which this water, fresh or salt, interacts with the land and its inhabitants will determine the future of the region. Like most of Florida, the region is flat. A rise in sea level of ten feet would submerge it. Marco Island, where consolidated sand dunes and old Indian mounds reach to over fifty feet in elevation, is the highest ground. The Ten Thousand Islands, in part, are formed on drowned sand dunes that mark an earlier shoreline from when sea levels were lower. If mean sea level were to drop four feet, most of them would again be connected to the mainland.

The Gulf coast of southern Florida is a mangrove coast. These trees are adapted to living in the fluctuating salinities and constantly changing water levels of the intertidal zone. They cannot become established below the mean low-tide level, where the ground is usually submerged, nor can they compete successfully with those species that can invade above the mean high-tide level where the ground is dry. They can tolerate fresh water or water with low salinity, but there they must compete with plants better adapted to fresh-water environments. For the most part, therefore, they are coastal fringe species and indicators both of fluctuating salinities and of ground that is flooded by the higher tides of each day. Since there are four separate species, however, that are known as mangroves in Florida, it is not possible to generalize too far.

The red mangrove is most tolerant of submersion, growing in areas that are exposed only by the lowest tides. Its tall, stiltlike aerial roots hold the body of the tree out of water and brace it against tidal movement and wave action. Black mangrove demands regular aeration of its roots, which are equipped with aerial projections that grow up through the mud, providing for the passage of oxygen and carbon dioxide into and out of the root system. It tends to occupy higher ground than the red mangrove. White mangrove has a similar adaptation for aeration of its roots, but it is less common and tends to occupy somewhat higher ground. The buttonwood, or button-mangrove, is actually not a mangrove at all, although it grows in close association with the others. Commonly it occupies dry ground or ground flooded by only the highest tides.

Mangroves have many peculiarities other than their affinity for the intertidal zone. They are, for the most part, made up of species that are not closely related botanically, but share a common habitat preference. Red mangrove (*Rhizophora mangle*) is the only Florida representative of the tropical mangrove family (*Rhizophoraceae*). As a species, it ranges widely in the North and South American tropics. White mangrove (*Laguncularia racemosa*) and buttonwood (*Conocarpus erectus*) belong to a family of woody plants (*Combretaceae*) that includes a great num-

The mangrove coast: red and black mangroves.

ber of species of such genera as *Terminalia* and *Combretum* that are widespread in the dry tropics of Africa, Asia, and the Americas. The black mangrove (*Avicennia nitida*) belongs to the verbena family (*Verbenaceae*), which includes such tropical woody plants as the East Indian teak and the ornamental lantana shrub. All these mangroves are indicators of the tropical influence on Florida's shores. The black mangrove is the most tolerant of cool weather, growing as far north as St. Augustine on the east and the Cedar Keys on the west. Buttonwood, red mangrove, and white mangrove are for the most part restricted to the area from Cape Kennedy or Tampa Bay southward.

The mangrove zone is important ecologically in many ways. Water moving toward the Gulf from the interior filters through the mangroves in a maze of minor and major channels. In place of a sudden outpouring of fresh water into an estuary following heavy rain in the interior, a more gentle, widely distributed flow moves through the mangrove jungles, carrying nutrients brought down from the interior or picked up during the slower movement through the swamps. The shock of a sudden change of salinity in the estuaries is thus reduced, and species that cannot stand such sudden shifts from saline to fresh water are spared. The myriad of pools and channels in the mangrove zone provide a haven for many species of juvenile fish, larval stages of the pink shrimp, and other invertebrates that require shelter and protection from enemies. Furthermore the growth and decay of the mangroves themselves bring nutrients from deeper in the soil to the surface. With leaf fall, or upon the death and decay of the mangroves, these nutrients are added to the waters of the mangrove zone. The fallen mangrove leaves themselves have been shown to be of great importance to the food chains that support the fisheries of southern Florida by research carried out at the University of Miami by William Odum and E. Heald. These leaves support an abundant growth of smaller attached algae and fungi that assist in the breakdown of the leaves and in turn provide food for a wide range of aquatic animals.

The mangrove zone becomes important economically as an area that can be dredged and filled to create shore-front real estate. The dredging of a network of canals surrounding the filled ground permits boat access to the backdoor of the homeowner who acquires and builds on a lot in the newly filled ground. The process of dredging and filling destroys not only the mangrove area, but the soils of the submerged land with their associated plant and animal life. Following dredging, some areas of bay bottom are scraped down to a barren and unproductive subsoil which ceases to support much life. Other areas are covered with silt washed from the filled land. The enriching, sheltering, and water-distributing effect of the mangrove swamp is removed. Runoff water from the new development pours through canals into estuaries or bays, resulting in sudden salinity changes that can in turn be destructive to aquatic life.

Politically the mangrove zone, along with all intertidal and submerged lands below the mean high-water mark, came under state ownership when Florida entered the Union, with the understanding that they would be held in trust until such time as they could be disposed of, or maintained, for the benefit of all the people of Florida. In practice, they came under the jurisdiction of the trustees of the Internal Improvement Fund, meaning the state cabinet. Operating under the assumption that the best way to benefit the people and improve Florida was to encourage settlement and development, this agency very willingly disposed of submerged lands. In 1856, a law was passed which permitted property owners to fill submerged lands in front of their waterfront property out as far as the edge of a navigable channel. Fortunately, in those early days the costs of dredging and filling and the low value of land prevented much activity. However, submerged lands were allowed to pass from public to private ownership at very little economic gain to the state.

After World War II, and particularly in the 1950s, the pressure to dredge and fill submerged and intertidal land in Florida grew intense. Fortunately, the state acted to reverse the law of 1856. In 1957, a Bulkhead Act was passed which reaffirmed state ownership of lands below the mean high-water mark. Public lands were no longer to be sold, and dredging from public lands or filling was restricted to such cases where the public interest was clearly involved. Permits were to be required for dredging and filling, and these required the approval of the county authorities, the state, and the United States Army Corps of Engineers (representing the federal interest in navigable waters). It would be naïve to assume that the passage of this act accomplished any great change. The public interest was broadly interpreted and permits were rarely withheld. In 1967, however, several changes for the better occurred. The Randall Act of the Florida legislature required that a biological survey, by the State Board of Conservation, precede the issuance of any state permit and that permits were to be withheld where biological values of importance would be endangered by dredging and filling. An agreement between the Department of the Interior and the Department of Defense provided that the United States Bureau of Sport Fisheries and Wildlife be consulted prior to the issuance of permits by the Army Corps of Engineers. The corps has subsequently refused permits where fish and wildlife values would be impaired, and this has led to a court battle to test the legality of the agreement. Although there are still many loopholes (after-the-fact permits are commonly issued to law violators after a nominal fine), laws are being tightened to protect the estuaries and intertidal lands of Florida.

But meanwhile, in southwestern Florida, great changes had taken place. Marco Island was being developed, Rookery Bay was threatened with development, and it seemed likely that the whole of the Ten Thousand Islands region might follow (the Collier County master plan showed them zoned for residential development, and a highway was sketched in to Key West running through the mangrove zone of Everglades National Park—its major wilderness region).

The movement of fresh water in southwestern Florida is of major concern to anyone who would either develop or protect land. Fresh water moves from the north and east toward the south and west, either in a generally sluggish surface flow or through underground aquifers. Most of the water for residential and urban purposes in southwestern Florida is derived from wells or well fields driven into a shallow surface aquifer, filled in part by water filtering into the limestone in the area of Hendry and Collier counties lying west and south of Lake Okeechobee. Here there are thousands of small lakes and ponds that fill in the wet season and often hold water throughout the year. Everglades City, in the Ten Thousand Islands region, is an exception to this general pattern. Its water is derived from the deeper Floridian aquifer which is recharged high in the central highlands. The surface water which flows from Lake Okeechobee into the Everglades does not normally move into the region of Naples or the northern Ten Thousand Islands.

In order to keep fresh water in the aquifers that supply human needs in Florida, it is necessary to keep a constant head of fresh water moving through them. If this is interrupted, salt water can invade the aquifers in their lower reaches and move inland. Thus, if too many wells are drilled and too much fresh water is removed, salt water will invade the well fields. If land is drained, to make it suitable for residential development, and if fresh water is then led directly through canals into the sea, the head of water in the aquifers is again reduced and salt water can invade. Furthermore, if sea-level canals, to create waterfront property and provide boat access to the Gulf, are constructed inland from the normal reaches of high tide, sea water can also be introduced into the aquifers at this level.

Since waterfront property with boat access is at a premium, developers often seek permission to construct canals going far inland. To protect the aquifers, most waterfront counties in Florida have established a salinity line, usually along the line marking the upper reaches of brackish, tidal water. In Collier County, an effort by real-estate developers to have the salinity line moved inland was defeated by efforts led by the Collier County Conservancy, soon after they had moved to acquire Rookery Bay. However, holding the salinity line firm increases the pressure to develop property lying seaward of this line. Much of the land surrounding the Rookery Bay sanctuary was in this category.

To protect Rookery Bay, therefore, it was not enough to buy the land surrounding the bay. Attention must also be paid to the land that lies inland over which or through which water moves to enter the bay. If this water flow were cut off through dikes and canals, the estuarine qualities of the bay area would be destroyed. It could become more saline than the Gulf, since evaporation proceeds more rapidly in the shallow bay than in the open Gulf. Creatures intolerant of high salinity would disappear. The nursery-ground function which estuaries perform, sheltering young or larval stages of species that inhabit the Gulf as adults, would be lost. Similarly, if diking and drainage canals were to lead to sudden outpourings of fresh water in the rainy season, disastrous results could also occur.

Perhaps most importantly, if water polluted by sewage,

pesticides, or excessive fertilizer were to enter the bay, the results could be even more drastic. Poisonous pollutants could destroy many forms of life. An excess of nitrate and phosphate could cause the blooms (major increases) of microscopic organisms which create the deadly "red tides" of the Florida coast.

Thus, to protect Rookery Bay, it is necessary to control the movement of fresh water into it, to maintain the seasonal variations in flow that existed before human activities modified the picture. It is also necessary to control the quality of this water. However, such control legally rests either in the hands of the owners of the lands above the sanctuary, or in those of the county or state authorities.

Rookery Bay Sanctuary is therefore, on a small scale, in the same position as Everglades National Park. To protect the park, the flow of water from Lake Okeechobee southward must be protected. However, the National Park Service cannot afford to buy nor can it as yet control the use of the land over which this water flows. Rookery Bay Sanctuary was acquired at a major cost to the many people who contributed to its purchase. One cannot expect them to be able to buy the much larger area of land lying upstream from the sanctuary also.

The dilemma of Rookery Bay seemed difficult to resolve until Bill Vines, then employed as Collier County planner (the first and, thus far, last man to hold this position—since his job was abolished when he made recommendations unfavorable to some major developers), developed a scheme for a boundary canal, which would separate the sanctuary from the land lying inland from it. At the same time, Dr. Clarence Idyll of the University of Miami came up with a similar plan for an interceptor-spreader canal to act as a buffer between estuarine areas and upland development. Such a canal could regulate and distribute the quantity of water entering the mangrove zone, but in itself it would not be adequate for complete protection. For this, the entire pattern of land-use inland to the sanctuary would have to be affected. For Rookery Bay, this meant that a large number of landowners, some small and some large, would have to be convinced that it was to their advantage to use their land in such a way that the sanctuary would be protected. It meant, also, that the county commissioners must be convinced that land-use zoning to encourage a high quality of land-use must be instituted and that random, unplanned development must be discouraged. To attempt this task, the Conservation Foundation, in 1967, decided to use the Rookery Bay area as a site for an environmental-planning demonstration project.

Working closely with the Collier County Conservancy, the Conservation Foundation agreed to employ Bill Vines as the local project planner and coordinator. Joel Kuperberg represented the Conservancy interests, and cooperation was maintained with the Audubon Society. Since it was apparent that the first requirement was to bring to bear all available biological knowledge, the School of Atmospheric and Marine Sciences of the University of Miami was brought into the project. Under the direction of Dr. Idyll, Dr. Durbin Tabb and Bernie Yokel came to work as project consultants. Drawing on years of study of similar problems in Everglades National Park and on earlier work at Rookery Bay, they were able to determine quickly the nature of the Rookery Bay ecosystem and the essential conditions required for its protection.

For a determination of wildlife values in the area, the

talents of Dr. William Robertson of Everglades National Park were made available, along with those of Jack Allen of the Audubon Society. Dr. Frank Craighead, of Homestead, the leading authority on south Florida vegetation, carried out a survey of the area. Thus, within a few months, the existing knowledge of the ecology of the Rookery Bay area was brought together.

Next it was essential to bring together experts on engineering and hydrology. The Florida State Board of Conservation, the U.S. Geological Survey, and private consultants contributed. The legal, economic, and real-estate development aspects of the project were next examined by appropriate experts. As a final step, all the information was brought together by Bill Vines and Ann Satterthwaite of the Conservation Foundation and used to sketch out the guidelines for development of the area and to provide a preliminary plan for such conservation-oriented development.

During the early stages of the project, the landowners of the area were invited to a meeting in which the purposes and methods of the study were discussed. They seemed interested in such free attention to their problems. At the completion of the study, when the plan was ready for presentation, an additional meeting of the landowners was held. In general, the attendance and response seemed enthusiastic. The larger landowners at least seemed convinced of the value of the effort.

In the fall of 1968, the Rookery Bay project report was published, with considerable publicity and fanfare. It was applauded widely among planners and their associations. It attracted great attention among both conservationists and developers in other parts of Florida. It would have been pleasant to say that all went well, that the landowners and developers fell into line and that the region was developed by the best conservation guidelines. If I had finished this book when I should have, in 1968, I would have issued such an optimistic forecast. But now we are in the 1970s. In fact, not much happened, except for some falling out among the conservationists, fortunately repaired. Or so it seemed for many long months.

Conservation groups, by tradition, are accustomed to fighting *against,* not to fighting *for.* They have usually opposed; they have not proposed. There is something frightening about "putting your money where your mouth is" and coming up with a plan for development that will work. It is easier to fight all development and go down in defeat, knowing that you were *good* and the others were *evil.* But somewhere along the line, it is necessary to learn that you cannot protect everything, that growth and development cannot be everywhere opposed, that somewhere there is a necessity for compromise. Similarly the developers must realize that they cannot forever go on with their plans for self-enrichment at the expense of the human environment, that somewhere they must compromise with those who say that quality is just as important as quantity, that nature must be preserved in order to preserve the human race. Those who fight for a "fast buck" and then run away to some more favored area must find that the places to which they had planned to retreat are also being developed by other advocates of the "fast buck.", Those who fight everywhere to save every inch of the natural environment must realize that a blending of the natural with the man-made is what permits human survival, and that they too are human.

At Rookery Bay, it is frightening for conservationists to

75

The dredges and bulldozers start their work.

Waterfront property with boat access is at a premium.

Continuous development spreads along the coast, out from Marco, out from Naples, on and on. . . .

start the bulldozers moving, knowing that their effects are almost irrevocable, in support of a scheme that represents only the best ecologically oriented guesswork. There are few certainties in dealing with the natural environment. Because of the inherent complexities of any ecological system, there is always a greater probability of failure than of complete success. Any real-estate developer with a conscience (and there are some) has felt a similar unease as he started the earth-moving on a project. But it is unusual for a conservationist to be in such a position.

In 1969, optimism for Rookery Bay was renewed. A Switzerland-based firm indicated a willingness to move ahead with development in accordance with the conservation-oriented plan. Negotiations started between this group and the two major landowners of the region. At the same time the federal government, acting through the Office of Water Resources Research, approved a long-range research study in the area, in the belief that the findings would be significant to other areas throughout the United States. This brought the marine science group from the University of Miami into the area once more. A research station was established on property bought by the Collier County Conservancy and provided for the use of the university. However, by 1970, optimism was again beginning to fade.

Early in 1970, the Marco Island Development Company, which had purchased the Johnson Bay Tract from the Collier Company, announced plans for a major real-estate development immediately adjacent to Rookery Bay on the south. The conservancy interests and the Rookery Bay study team immediately met with the company to achieve safeguards for the sanctuary in this proposed development. The company expressed a willingness to build a wide range of conservation-oriented activities into their development plans and to seek ecological guidelines in order to prevent serious disruption of the aquatic ecosystems in their area. Nevertheless, as the plans were unfolded, it was obvious that not just the area next to Johnson Bay, but the entire region, shore and islands, from Rookery Bay southward to Cape Romano, was to be included in Marco Island developments.

Whereas the willingness of the Mackle Brothers, who controlled the Marco Island company, to make use of the best ecological advice was encouraging, and reflected the value of the work that had been done at Rookery Bay, it hardly compensated for the loss of the wild land and water southward from the bay and including some of the largest of the Ten Thousand Islands group—Kice Island and Cape Romano. The decision to protect this area in a natural state, although discussed by the American islands study team of the Department of the Interior as well as in proposals for aquatic reserves presented to the Florida state legislature, had not been made in time by either federal or state authorities.

Northward from Naples, further effects of the Rookery Bay plan were felt when a Miami developer announced his intention to develop his Black Island property in accordance with Rookery Bay guidelines. One could have been cheered by this news had not it signaled almost-continuous development from Naples to Fort Myers and beyond.

Around Rookery Bay itself, plans for developing Cannon Island and Little Marco Island, southwest of the bay, were being drawn up. Landowners on Key Island were once again pressuring for a road to their property. Developments moving southward from Naples were pressing down the Intracoastal Waterway toward the bay. Upstream on Henderson Creek, a series of small trailer courts contributed sewage effluent from faulty septic tanks and from the small sewage treatment units that they had been required to install. Adequate protection against water pollution in the county, outside of the city of Naples, seemed unavailable. The land in the Rookery Bay watershed seemed about to be slowly nibbled away by the kind of random activity and uncontrolled development that the Rookery Bay plan was intended to forestall. The county government remained without any meaningful plan for county development, without any set of environmental guidelines to aid in their control of growth and development, and seemed little inclined to develop either environmental planning or a system of zoning aimed at protection of the environment.

In this decade, one can still take a boat south from Naples and move quietly through the mangrove-lined channels or pull up on a palm-studded island. All around, blue herons and white egrets will be feeding, and an osprey can be seen wheeling overhead. A rookery of Louisiana herons and little blue herons has come back to the bay, and brown pelicans in hundreds roost on some of the smaller islands. Rookery Bay still looks serene and secure; there is nowhere a sign that its wildness is threatened. But development plans don't show up on the ground until the bulldozers start moving. Away from the mangrove fringe, the bulldozers have started to move. The sanctuary may still be saved, being valued in the future as a small sample of what used to be available everywhere and to everyone in this part of Florida. But those who want to save wilderness had best move on to somewhere else. This wilderness is on the way out. One wonders just where is "somewhere else"?

Alligator

5 : *An Ecosystem Enters Politics*

IT IS DIFFICULT to write about the Everglades without becoming emotional and sounding trite. So much has already been said. There have been an outpouring of passionate speeches and a burgeoning of articles that describe the wonders of this region and the dangers that beset it. In some ways the Everglades have been oversold, and many visitors may well be disappointed. Yet, there it stands—one of the great wilderness areas in the United States, and the only extensive tropical wilderness in the nation. It is a home for some of the nation's most valued and rare wildlife. There is no place like it; its scientific value alone is immeasurable; but, nevertheless, we persist in efforts that will eventually destroy it.

There is no grandeur to the Everglades in the sense that

one encounters in our mountain national parks. There is little of the intimate charm of the landscapes of northeastern America. The feeling that I associate with this region is more akin to that encountered in the wilder prairies of the West, the great sweeps of grass and sky, here mixed with equally broad horizons of water and endless marches of mangroves. It takes skill to capture this with a camera. Most photographs divide into two halves at the horizon, blue above and green below. I suspect that some internal receptivity must already exist in the visitor if he is to appreciate this country. But, if it is there, the Everglades become an exciting place of which one does not easily tire. The variety that exists is found, not in the broad landscape, but closer at hand—in the incredible complexity of a hammock forest

More akin to the wilder prairies of the west.

where it may be difficult for anyone but an expert in tropical trees to identify the dozens of woody species and where other kinds of experts are needed to name the countless species of herbs or air plants or the almost infinite array of insects; on the edge of a slough where you may see more kinds of water birds than you had believed existed, not to mention fish, turtles, and alligators; in the mangroves by the edge of the sea and the seascape dotted with islands; in the winding mystery of the maze of channels that move through the mangrove jungles where you cannot anticipate the wildlife you may encounter around every bend.

But the Everglades today are less a reality than an abstraction. They are the red flag waved in front of the development bull. He has charged, and has been frustrated— thus far. He is only beginning to grasp, in his apparently feeble brain, the reason why. People keep shouting, "Ecosystem, ecosystem!" at him. The word does not entirely register but dimly seems important. In the Everglades, an ecosystem entered politics.

To the tired armies of conservation, the Everglades jetport battle seemed just too much. They had been fighting on the Keys and the Ten Thousand Islands, on the Cross-Florida Barge Canal, and on the Suwannee. Suddenly, from nowhere apparently, a political entity that most had never heard of, the Dade County Port Authority, came forth with a plan to park a supersonic, transatlantic jetport right on the edge of Everglades National Park. The conservationists felt that surely they had fought enough for the Everglades—against the army engineers and the Flood Control District (both suddenly transformed into allies). It hardly seemed fair to have to gird for battle again. Besides, it all seemed incredible—they had thought that the whole idea of the supersonic transport, the great noisemaker, had been put to rest.

I doubt that the conservation forces could have fully rallied if the opposition, the spokesmen for the Dade County Port Authority, had not been both arrogant and stupid. In all their advance planning, done apparently in secrecy, they had not given more than a passing thought to the realities of the Florida environment. The word *ecology,* which they must sometime have heard, had not registered. Conservation, in their minds, had to do with a group of powerless nuts: "butterfly chasers" and "yellow-bellied sap-suckers." The good old Florida development pattern, based on the pursuit of the great green dollar by all the little men who cannot see the world around them, was to be followed. It was expected that, as usual, with the waving of a few million-dollar banners here and there, all opposition would be overcome and that the great machine labeled progress, with its wake of utter destruction, would roll forward according to plan.

For the conservationists, the first word of any trouble came with a *New York Times* news report describing the proposed jetport. It was to be located just inside the Big Cypress Swamp, at the edge of the Everglades proper, immediately north of the Tamiami Trail and just outside the national park. It was already being presented as a *fait accompli*—the decision had been made—it was too late to argue. Covering 39 square miles, its landing strips would serve not only to train jet pilots, but would eventually accommodate the giant supersonic transports, which could disseminate their sonic booms over the "useless and empty swamps" of Everglades National Park after their voyages from across the world. It was to be the great southern Florida jetport, replacing not only the Miami International Airport, but also serving, through a system of rapid transport to be devised, the whole region from Tampa and Palm Beach to the Keys. It was surely a bait worth rising to for any county commissioner, landowner, taxpayer, or would-be developer. In no time at all there would arise, according to the boosters, a city of half a million, perhaps even a million, in what had been "worthless wilderness." All that had been ignored in such forecasts was the national interest and environmental reality.

Those who cared about the environment were at first too stunned to respond. As one who went about waving the news in front of representatives of the National Park Service and various Florida conservation groups, I was surprised by the lack of attention. The attitude I encountered was one of skepticism, or of fatalism. Either the article was a mistake, and the decision would not be made until a much later date, or the whole thing was inevitable. The you-can't-fight-progress syndrome was clearly in evidence.

Indeed the whole thing was nearly inevitable. The bulldozers were ready to roll almost before the news had reached the public. The necessary land had been quietly purchased by those who knew. Before the argument had been fairly joined, it appeared to be over. It seemed appropriate to argue only about what was left and how to alleviate the damage. But then there was the presidential election and a change of teams at the higher levels of resource administration. Perhaps those who had made compromises in the past gave way to those who had no past commitments —these things are hard to know. Whatever it was, the National Park Service got up out of its supine position and came out fighting.

For the benefit of those who have only recently come in on this controversy, it is worth reviewing. Everglades National Park rests at the southern end of the Florida peninsula. It is, as one of the park service people has termed it, a "disarticulated ecosystem," since it is separated from the total environment on which it depends. In order to continue to exist, the national park must have a continued flow of water from the northward, from Lake Okeechobee and beyond, moving across the land surface as the wet season comes to an end, carrying moisture into the far reaches of the park and on into the estuaries of the Gulf and Florida Bay. The park also requires a subterranean flow of water to replenish the ground water and the springs and seeps within the park. The life of the park depends upon this water's being relatively pure, uncontaminated with the poisons which, under the name of pesticides, man has seen fit to turn loose in his environment.

The water that the park requires originates on and flows through lands that are not directly under the control of the federal government, even though the Army Corps of Engineers has played a major role in their development. South of Lake Okeechobee, and to some extent north of it, the lands are under the control of the Central and Southern Florida Flood Control District. For many years the name of this agency had been anathema to those interested in the long-term future of the human environment, since its leaders seemed unable to see beyond the immediate needs of agriculture, flood control, and urban water supply. But with the election of Claude Kirk as governor of Florida, the personnel had changed. The chairman became Robert Padrick, ostensibly only an automobile man from Fort Pierce, but in operation one of the more effective conservationists that Florida has seen. Ranging beyond what might have been expected, he had joined with Bill Partington of the Florida Audubon Society in proposing a Florida state wilderness system, to include significant portions of the Everglades conservation areas that were under control of the flood control district.

During the drought years of the early 1960s, it appeared that Everglades National Park would dry up and burn away. Its aquatic ecosystems, cut off from their Okeechobee water supply by the dikes and canals of the flood control district, seemed likely to become barren, dry-land environments inhabited by little life. The battle for Everglades water was fought in the newspapers and journals, in the state legislature and in Congress, over difficult months and years. Suddenly, with Kirk and Padrick and a new attitude on the part of the Corps of Engineers, it became possible for an agreement to be reached between the Department of the Interior and the Corps of Engineers under which

On the edge of a slough.

315,000 acre-feet of water, at a minimum, would be provided each year to the national park. This was deemed by the National Park Service to be the minimum flow that would sustain the life systems of the glades and the fisheries and waterfowl of the estuaries. Unfortunately, the agreement was not a long-term guarantee of water. There was the possibility that future drought years, and increasing demands from Miami and the farming lands, might lead to its revocation. But 1968 and 1969 were high rainfall years. A surplus rather than a deficiency of water presented a problem. The water crisis seemed over. But then came the jetport and other depressing news.

It has been difficult for most conservationists who favor parks and sanctuaries to understand the full message being broadcast by ecologists and others interested in the total environment. Too often the National Park Service retires behind its park boundaries and is content, finding enough to do with managing visitors, providing roads, trails, and campgrounds, and answering its own memoranda. Too often, the private conservationists, having spearheaded a drive to set aside a park or purchase land for a reserve, retire upon their laurels, feeling that they have done their bit for conservation. This is almost good enough when the land set aside or purchased is on top of a mountain. It is an unfortunate attitude when the land is at the bottom of a watershed and dependent upon the whim of those who live upstream.

On the upper reaches of the Everglades water system is agricultural land. For this discussion, it perhaps is not significant that it is misplaced agricultural land, where farming eats its way down through its soil capital exposed by land clearing and drainage to the oxidation caused by tropical sun, rain, and subsequent bacterial action—working its way to extinction and exhaustion in a matter of decades at best. The agriculture is nevertheless there, highly profitable at present for the farmers, who in their efforts have depended here, as everywhere, upon the assistance of fertilizers and pesticides.

Down in the national park, the rangers had talked with pride about their bald eagles and ospreys, survivors from a once widespread population, their brown pelicans, wood storks, limpkins, and other rare birds. But then the pesticides began to drift southward, carried by Okeechobee water or borne by air currents from the north. It was not until 1968 that the alarm was really sounded. The protected birds of the national park began showing the symptoms, thin egg shells and other interferences with reproduction, previously noted among all those species high on food chains, hawks and fish-eaters, farther to the north. Pesti-

They pointed with pride to their pelicans.

cides, particularly the chlorinated hydrocarbon group, including DDT, appeared to be about to take their toll. The National Park Service began to consider ways and means to guarantee the continued flow of pesticide-free water, and air, for the park. Then came the news of the jetport and the prospect of a major urban area contributing its poisons and wastes to the waters moving through the park.

People in Florida and elsewhere had fought hard to establish Everglades National Park. It was first discussed in the 1920s when the Florida developers were having their first unimpeded victories and were talking bravely of draining all the Everglades once and forever. Even then, however, there were some who thought that Florida should offer more than coast-to-coast residential lots and highways. They began the effort to have part of the Everglades protected. It was not, however, until after World War II that any degree of success was forthcoming. In 1948, Congress voted and President Truman dedicated Everglades National Park—dedicated the area on the map, but failed to provide money to buy all the land within its boundaries and failed to provide any guarantee of the water needed for its survival. But in fairness, at that time any real pressure upon Everglades land or water seemed a remote prospect. The earlier development efforts had failed. Those who dedicated the park had scarcely heard of the population explosion that had already begun.

I don't want to recall here the entire story of the Everglades and its ecology, already told so ably by Marjorie Stoneman Douglas in her *Everglades—River of Grass* and more briefly by Bill Robertson in his *Everglades—The Park Story,* but there are some points that need be stressed. The Everglades are dependent not just on total quantity of water. The water must be free from pesticides or other poisons, from excessive fertilizers, sewage, or their derivatives. They are also dependent on seasonality of water, the amount that arrives at a particular time of year. Most of the fresh-water plants of the Everglades cannot stand continual submergence any more than they can stand continued drought. Frank Craighead found, on examining the tree islands in and around Shark River slough, that the excess of water coming from the flood control district, following the heavy rains of 1968, had done almost as much damage as the earlier drought. Trees that normally stood high and dry on hammocks had their roots submerged and were dying as a consequence. Animals, such as deer and raccoons, that depended on tree islands during the flood season, were lost when the islands on which they had found sanctuary were submerged. Strangely, even the alligators, badly hit by the preceding drought, were being drowned out. The nest mounds on which their eggs were laid and incubated were submerged or eroded away by the excess of water.

Problems of flood and drought did not originate with man's activities. The Everglades were adapted to lean years and fat years. But the problems were exacerbated by man's activities, starting with the aftermath of the 1920s hurricanes, when the southward flow of water was first interrupted in a massive way. Next came the Tamiami Trail, a dike across the glades through which only a limited number of culverts and channels penetrated. Then came the flood control district's dikes, canals, and flood-control structures; then, an even more massive barrier in the major highway "Alligator Alley" across the northern glades. What had been an even and dispersed southward movement of water

Even the alligators were being drowned out.

across a broad surface was canalized and directed. Much of the flow into the park, for example, came through flood control gates under the Tamiami Trail into Shark River slough. In high-water years, this appeared to be too much. In drought years, areas away from the water-diversion structures suffered from dryness.

Within the park itself, there were major problems. Craighead investigated the balance between fresh water and salt along the mangrove rim of the park on the west and south. He found that a natural barrier, formed when sea levels were higher, built in part of mangrove peat, had impeded the seaward movement of fresh water over the surface and blocked the inward movement of salt water. When this barrier was breached by canals or burned out by fires, sea water came farther into the glades and fresh water drained out more quickly. By the time of Craighead's investigations in the 1960s, the ecology of the park had been drastically modified from that which had existed during the 1930s.

Investigation of the animal life in the park produced depressing results. The pressure to establish a national park in this region was brought, in part, because of the existence of a fantastic array of bird life in the region. The need to preserve roseate spoonbills, egrets, white herons, blue herons, bald eagles, brown pelicans, ospreys, limpkins, and dozens of other species was part of the reason for setting aside the park. But since the park was established, the record of conservation is erratic indeed. Part of the reason is illustrated by consideration of one species.

The wood stork, once known as the wood ibis, a strange, ungainly bird on the ground, but a vision of the spirit of wilderness in its flight, is a good example of the ways things are tied together by the bonds of nature. The stork nests in the Everglades, in the Audubon Society's Corkscrew Swamp, and in a few other places. No great strain is involved in protecting its nesting sites from those who would plunder. But young storks must be fed, and to do this, the parents must forage into those areas in which fish are concentrated. These concentrations are provided through the drying out of the glades or swamps in late winter. If the storks find such food and the young are reared, they will then disperse out of the parks and reserves to spend the summer in a variety of places in Florida and along the Gulf coast. Here they are dependent on the good will and land-use sense of a large segment of America's human population. The storks need clusters of tall trees for roosting and swamps and waterways for feeding. They cannot survive in areas entirely cleared for farms or residences. They depend on at least some reasonable interspersion of wild land and tame and on some reasonable interest in their survival. No park, however large, can contain them. America is their home, and the attitude of Americans towards nature, their only guarantee for the future.

In Everglades National Park in the 1960s, it was found that those species dependent upon bays and estuaries, previously depleted by plume hunters and other forms of predation, had increased and recovered splendidly. The spoonbills and great white herons illustrated this recovery. The population of those species dependent primarily on fresh water, however, including the wood stork and limpkin, and outside of the park the Everglades kite, had gone steadily down. Depletion of the fresh-water environment and of all the small and large aquatic life dependent upon it appeared to be the reason. Finally, of course, with the growing movement of pesticides into fresh and salt water alike, the future of all species was in danger. There were an estimated 1.5 million colonial water birds in Everglades National Park when it was first considered for park status. There were perhaps fifty thousand in the late 1960s. The good will and land-use sense of the American people have obviously been inadequate.

Perhaps somewhere along the line, a lesson should be learned—one cannot preserve part of an ecosystem without attending to all of it. It must be recognized that one can't preserve a plant-eating animal without saving the plants on which it feeds. One can't preserve these without saving the soil, the water, the atmosphere, the sunlight, on which they depend. An ecosystem is a unity. It cannot be

93

subdivided unless one is prepared to come forth with a workable substitute for each of its parts. Otherwise it ceases to function. This must be learned if man is to survive. Perhaps the Everglades are a good place to teach the lesson.

To return to the jetport. When the Department of the Interior and the various citizen conservation groups finally took on the battle in early 1969, the bulldozers were already in action. While the controversy went on, clearings were made through the Big Cypress Swamp and the first landing strip, a jet training strip, was gouged out of the wilderness. The federal government was apparently powerless, and its agencies, the Federal Aviation Authority and Bureau of Public Roads in the Department of Transportation, and the Department of the Interior, were hardly in agreement. Nevertheless, the development of the jetport was dependent upon the cooperation of the Department of Transportation; it was dependent upon the building of Interstate Highway 75 as a major freeway across from Tampa and upon the development of a better highway and transit system from the jetport to Miami.

The Department of the Interior moved effectively, sending Luna Leopold of the U.S. Geological Survey to head a team of experts looking into the effects of the jetport on the ecology of the region. The National Academy of Sciences came into the act with a similar study by a team headed by Gordon MacDonald. Reports from both agencies became available in autumn of 1969. Both were in general agreement. Faced with the facts and confronted by an overwhelming public opposition to the construction of the jetport, the administration took action. The Secretary of the Interior, Walter Hickel, and of Transportation, John Volpe, jointly announced their opposition to the jetport and their unwillingness to contribute to its support and construction. Florida papers headlined the event. The Florida developers were stunned. But they were not yet defeated. They still had their jet training strip, and still had hope that the tide of opinion could be turned. The *coup de grace* was not given until January, 1970, when President Nixon announced not only that the jetport location must be permanently abandoned, but that the training strip must also be located with the future jetport whenever a suitable location for this was established—away from the Everglades. It is worth noting that by this time, the Dade County Port Authority had expended $14 million on the planning and preliminary development of the Everglades jetport, so sure were they that the conservation opposition could be overcome. Never before in American history had development been stopped in the name of conservation, when development was already so far advanced. It was a time to be remembered—for both sides.

There was other good news for the Everglades. Late in 1969, the pesticides controversy had boiled over. The use of DDT and its relatives had been halted or greatly restricted by federal and state action, although not completely prevented. It seemed likely that the drift of poisons from the north into the Everglades might taper off and finally stop.

With so many victories, the forces of conservation began to retire from the field. But this rest can only be for a brief time. The battle went well, but the war is not yet won. So long as the pressure of population, the demand for development, the concept that profit is best made at the expense of the natural environment remain active in the field, one can only brace oneself for future effort. The Everglades may yet be permanently and irrevocably lost, but they must not be lost without a life-and-death struggle. The survival of all mankind may rest in the balance, not because the human race depends upon the Everglades, but because it must learn the lesson that the Everglades can teach and learn it now.

Pelicans

6 : A String of Little Islands

IN A CHAIN that extends southward off the coast from Miami, ending finally northward from Cuba in the Dry Tortugas, is the most attractive string of islands to be found within the continental waters of the United States. On one side are the opalescent waters of Florida Bay, merging through mangrove-rimmed sounds with those of Biscayne Bay on the north. On the other are the brilliant green waters of Hawk Channel and Turtle Harbor Channel which separate the Keys from the long reef of living coral that forms their outer boundary. Beyond the reef rolls the deep and violet-blue water of the Gulf Stream. There, where the rocks and coral heads bear the names of ships that they have sent to the bottom, is the edge of Florida and of the North American continent. Inward the shallow waters have come and gone with the rising and falling of the sea in past glacial ages. Seaward has always been the ocean, falling off rapidly down the continental slope to abyssal depths.

To one who has followed the early history of the West Indies and Florida, many of the names of these islands have a magic sound—Key Largo and Matecumbe, Indian Key and Tea Table Key, Big Pine Key and Key West. Each has its tale of pirates or wreckers, of Spanish galleons, French and English corsairs, Indian wars and naval exploits. Viewed from the air, the Keys, white-rimmed with sand, edged with coral or fringed with mangroves, stood out once as dark green gems of tropical verdure against the brilliance of the sea. Viewed from the air today, they tell a different story—one of dredged bottoms and the glaring white silt of filled land, of bulldozed acres, and of development proceeding without thought of or care for the values of islands or forests or seas.

An island is by definition a body of land completely surrounded by water. One travels to an island over water, by boat or raft, by swimming if necessary, or in more modern days, by air. Living on an island, therefore, makes one feel cut off, separated from all other land by that water barrier. To some, that feeling of separateness, that island feeling, has unbelievable value and adds an entire dimension to life. These are the island people. But all people who come to islands are not island people. Some come through no love of islands, but only love of money. To these, and to others of diverse motives, the quality of islandness is without value. Profits are enhanced when accessibility is increased, when those who do not really like islands can be encouraged to settle on them by removing the fear of being cut off. It is these people, and not the islanders, who have prevailed. They work hard for their goals, while islanders often want only to be left alone.

And so the Florida Keys of the magic names, from Largo down the chain to Key West, are islands no more. Those who wanted to get to Key West fast or to haul more goods more quickly back and forth from Miami or to sell land to people who were not island people have won out. A new peninsula has been formed, one held together for a time by only two thin lines of steel rails, but joined now and perhaps forever by the solid concrete of highway construction. Now you can get there fast and get away fast, and it all looks more and more like Miami. Unless you pay close attention, you may never know that the islands once were there.

But roads have not gone everywhere yet. Beyond Key West are the Marquesas and the remote Dry Tortugas. North of the highway are the separate islands of Florida Bay, some saved by Everglades National Park, others under government ownership as part of the Great White Heron or Key Deer wildlife refuges. From Key Largo north are separate islands that will remain that way as a part of the new Biscayne National Monument. Thus there is still hope for those who like islands, and on the main line of Keys, it is still possible to create a way of living of an excellence unique in America.

The Florida Keys are not a single archipelago of uniform origin. The upper keys, extending as far west as Key Vaca, are an old coral reef, formed when sea levels were much higher than today. The lower keys, from Big Pine to Key West, are of separate origin, part of the Miami oolite formation, limestone laid down under the sea during the

A new peninsula has been formed.

There are still the separate islands of Florida Bay.

high waters of interglacial times. Still other islands are of more recent biological origin, accumulations of mud and sand built up in bars where mangroves could then colonize, with soils formed and added to by generations of growing plants, enriched by bird droppings and sometimes by the midden heaps of Indian occupancy. All the Keys are low and flat—twenty feet in elevation would seem a mountainous height. Only the forest vegetation gives them profile and protection from hurricane winds and surging seas.

Biologically, the Keys are much more thoroughly tropical and West Indian than any other part of Florida. Of the tropical trees that find a home in Florida, more than one-

Florida Keys.

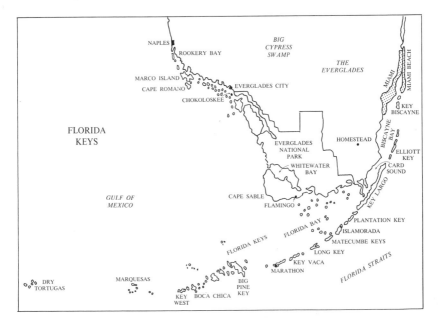

third are found only on the Keys, and approximately two-thirds are found only in the area from Miami and Marco Island southward through the Keys. Early visitors to the Keys described the tall tropical woodlands that grew there. Now only patchy remnants of these forests can be found. Man's activities alone, or the aid which they give to the destructive forces of hurricanes, have led to the disappearance of the old woods. An island forest is an ecological entity, built up in adaptation to the natural forces of the environment. Where undisturbed, the Key forests would have a dome-shaped profile reaching from the sea-level growth of mangroves or the wind-shaped beach shrubs to the tallest trees in the protected interior of the island. Such a profile, and the solid phalanxes of vegetation surrounding the older, interior woods, gives protection against winds. But let the edges be cut away or clearings created in the middle or roads carved through the island woodland and wind channels are created—areas of eddying where the destructive forces of winds can reach the formerly sheltered trees.

The Keys formed a home also for the more tropical animal life of Florida. There flamingos once lived, visiting from the Bahamas or Cuba, and at one time breeding on Sugarloaf Key and perhaps on others. But that was before human activities reduced their numbers and removed them from the list of native Florida residents. The roseate spoonbill held out on the Keys after it had disappeared from the rest of Florida. Bottlepoint Key, just north of Key Largo, was their last known breeding ground when they reached their low ebb during the early 1940s. Since then they have recovered and moved out over their original range.

The Keys are the center for the great white heron, the largest bird of its kind. Reduced by hunting, these herons were pushed to the point of extinction by the 1935 hurricane. Since then, under protection, they too have recovered their numbers. In the Keys also is the only United States nesting ground for the large white-crowned pigeon, a bird that had been cut down by steady pothunting in the early days of the Keys and is now endangered both by loss of its forest habitat and by continued pothunting in its winter home in the Bahamas. In the Keys also one may see such West Indian birds as the scissor-tailed flycatcher, the mangrove cuckoo, the bananaquit, the scaled pigeon, and the zenaida dove.

The Keys are the only home of the key deer, the pygmy whitetail which at some time in the past migrated to the outer keys and has been confined to them since. Hunting and later habitat destruction reduced their numbers, exterminating them on most islands. They too, with adequate protection, have regained lost ground.

In more desperate straits is the only population of crocodiles in the United States. Most persons believe that there are only about twenty of these left, confined mostly to national park waters in Florida Bay in the vicinity of Key Largo.

Very likely the Keys have been inhabited by man almost as long as they have been above the surface of the ocean. The Indians that were in the Keys at the dawn of written history are generally called Matecumbes, although many writers confuse them with the Calusas, the Indians of the formidable Chief Carlos of the Gulf Coast. Like the other Florida Indians, they were warlike from the start and gave short shrift to would-be invaders from Spain. After the days of Ponce de León, most Spaniards did not visit the Keys intentionally, but came through the workings of fate in the shapes of unsuspected coral reefs. Many a treasure ship, homeward bound on the Gulf Stream from the Indies or Latin America, reached the end of its journey on some unnamed coral head. The crew, if it survived, was killed on the spot or herded away to be disposed of at some more ceremonial occasion.

Rarely, a captive was kept and adopted by the tribe. Such was Hernando d'Escalante Fontaneda, a youth at the time of his capture, who was to live as an Indian for 17 years. His memoirs have given us some picture of Indian life before it was modified by European influence. But his writing is colored by the intense and enduring hatred he had for his captors. He could see the Indians as subjects fit only for utter extermination. For a time, however, fate willed otherwise, and the only extermination victims were the luckless Spaniards whose ships ran aground.

As happened elsewhere in the Americas, the diseases of Europe conquered in time where Spanish arms had failed. Hit by epidemics to which they had no immunity, the Key Indians dwindled in strength and numbers. It is hard to know what finally happened. The Calusas from the Gulf Coast were to come to the Keys during the eighteenth century. Later, Seminole raiding parties were frequent visitors. It is thought that some of the original Indians, learning after encounters with British and Americans to view the Spanish as friends, fled to Havana where they ultimately vanished as a people.

The Indians were the Keys' first wreckers and built a way of life that was to continue later in other hands. Certainly during the eighteenth century, the Keys were a home for a mixed lot of wreckers, pirates, and refugee Indians. They are rich with pirate legends, but most of these are more fancy than fact. Piracy was ultimately brought to a halt when the United States took over Florida. In 1822, Commodore David Porter arrived in Key West with a naval squadron for the purpose of eliminating the pirates and making the straits and the Gulf safe for shipping. After some bloody battles, the days of Blackbeard and Black Caesar, of José Gaspar, Tavernier, and all the other buccaneers, real or imaginary, came to an end.

But the wreckers, mostly pursuing an honest trade, remained in business. In 1828, Congress established a federal court at Key West to handle the various salvage claims of those who harvested that bounty from the sea—the cargo from ships that had smashed into the coral. In the 1830s, wrecking vessels were moved down from Mystic, Connecticut, to take advantage of the lucrative salvage trade of the Keys, but even greater numbers of wreckers came from the Bahamas. These were the Conchs, Bahama settlers of British origin, some descended from the Loyalists who had fled the United States during the Revolutionary War. These people, named after the large shellfish that was a staple article in their diet, were to provide an island-oriented, sea-going group of colonists for the Keys.

The Conchs were joined in Key West, increasingly, by refugees from Spanish Cuba. These were to make the town a center for cigar making in the United States during the nineteenth century. The relationship of the Keys and of Florida to Cuba was to be established as early as the 1840s. At that time the first attempt to liberate Cuba from Spanish rule was launched from Key West under the leadership of Colonel Narcisso Lopez. It was unsuccessful, but subsequently Cuban refugees were to come to the Keys in greater numbers. In the 1890s, José Marti, who was to become liberator of Cuba, operated from Key West. In 1895, he started the revolution that ended with the Spanish–American War and Spanish defeat. Still later, the Keys were to receive refugees from Batista's dictatorship, and today the boats that carry refugees from Communist Cuba still come ashore. But today the axis between Key West and Havana has been broken, and the special relationship of trade and tourism that tied Florida and Cuba together has ceased to exist. Only hijacked planes make the journey across to Havana. Only the most desperate escapees from Castro's red island now dare to cross the 90 miles of the Florida straits.

In the early 1900s, railroad men were a powerful breed in America. One of the most famous of these was Henry Flagler, who was determined to tie the Florida east coast together by rail. Operating against what most people considered to be common sense, he pushed the rail lines south from Jacksonville to Palm Beach, then on to Miami at a time when it seemed unlikely to become more than a small town. Most would have given up at this point, but Flagler was driven to go southward to the farthest limits of the nation. Starting in 1905, his men moved from island to island with their rails, fighting hurricanes and hardships, bridging the long water gaps that separated the outer Keys. In 1912, his first train rolled into Key West, and the "railroad that went to sea" was complete. For 23 years, it functioned until it was hammered to death by the 1935 hurricane. The Keys for a time became islands once more. By 1938, however, the overseas highway, following and using the old railway right of way and Flagler's railway bridges, was completed to Key West. It remains today one of America's most spectacular roadways.

Even after the days when the establishment of navigational aids and the development of more manageable ships brought the wrecking business to an end, the people of the Keys were oriented seaward and depended upon the ocean for much of their support. Sponge beds existed off Key West, and the Conch settlers took up sponge fishing as early as the 1840s. For a long time sponges remained profitable, but by the late nineteenth century, competition from the Tarpon Springs spongers and the depredations of a disease that attacked the local sponge populations largely finished the Key West business.

A sea-turtle fishery was developed early in the history of the Keys. Green turtles from the Grand Caymans and Central America were brought to Key West by turtle schooners and held there in turtle corrals. Loggerheads, home-grown on the Keys, were also captured, and other species of sea turtles were gathered from here and there. Turtle steaks and turtle soup became standard, if choice, fare on the Florida Keys. Unfortunately the business continued as its biological base was eroded away. All the sea turtles are today in some degree endangered both from damage to their nesting beaches and excessive killing of the adults. A major program launched through the leadership of Dr. Archie Carr of the University of Florida is aimed at their protection and restoration, but more restrictive laws for their protection are also needed.

Sea fisheries remain of great importance to the Keys, but the value of the sport fishery now far overrides that of the commercial take. An exception to this is the pink-shrimp fishery which came into existence in the 1950s. The major shrimping ground is in a broad region north of the Dry Tortugas. Here hundreds of shrimp boats operate—from the Keys, from other Florida ports, and from ports around the Gulf. The value of the catch was over $16 million in 1965 and competes with the salmon and tuna fisheries for first place among the nation's fisheries. However, the Tortugas' beds support only the adult shrimp. For a long time it was not known where these adults came from. In the 1960s, University of Miami scientists discovered that the larval and postlarval shrimp migrate to the estuaries on the Gulf coast of Everglades National Park. Here in these plankton-rich waters, protected by mangrove swamps, they rapidly grow in size and as juveniles migrate back to sea to join the adults in the Dry Tortugas' beds. Thus the entire shrimp fishery, which could be capitalized at over a billion dollars, is dependent upon the care given to the land and water of the Everglades ecosystem.

Despite the seaward orientation of the Key dwellers, use of the land for a multitude of purposes has also gone on. During their early period of isolation, the inhabitants strove toward some degree of self-sufficiency, attempting to supplement their diet of seafood with agricultural produce. Undoubtedly one of the first food crops was the *Zamia* plant, a low-growing palmlike relative of the ornamental cycads from the fleshy roots of which the Indian bread *coontie* was made. These roots, like those of Asian sago, are rich in starch, which when pounded out and washed, becomes suitable as flour. The Keys support most tropical fruit trees, but except for the famous Key limes, have never been a center for the citrus industry. In the nineteenth century, pineapples and limes were produced commercially and in quantity, but these crops were not able to compete against crops from other areas, nor has agriculture in general held up well against the demand for land for other purposes.

The elements of change operating on the Keys have long since modified their vegetation from what existed in presettlement days. Such timber trees as mahogany, mastic, and lignum vitae were sought after for their high-value woods. The common buttonwood, in the mangrove group, was cut down for fuel and charcoal in the days before coal and petroleum became generally available. The other mangroves were occasionally cut down for their tanning bark. Clearing for agriculture and then for housing modified considerable areas of the Keys even before the recent flood of people into this region. Nevertheless, up to the time of

An imaginative program preserved the old quarter of Key West.

World War II, most of the Keys were in natural vegetation and had recovered from earlier changes. Allen Andrews has described a trip to Key West in 1938 in which he noted that a dense forest hemmed in the road on both sides as he drove the length of Key Largo. It was broken only by an occasional lime grove or filling station. Tavernier was the only town of importance outside of Key West. Little real-estate development was in evidence, and Key West was almost entirely an eighteenth- to nineteenth-century city. The contrast with today is apparent.

Little undisturbed forest now remains on the road to Key West. Highway strip development is everywhere. Only a major effort on the part of Key West citizens, and an imaginative program of restoration by the federal government during the New Deal period, has managed to preserve the fascinating old quarter of that city. This is now surrounded entirely by what are mostly unimaginative and often depressing modern developments. More upsetting is the realization that development is accelerating and that little or no effort is being extended to realize the potential that the Keys offer as one of the most attractive areas for human residence to be found in America.

Deer in Pines

7 : A String of Little Victories

NOBODY WITH ANY SORT of a conscience can just sit by and watch the Keys being ruined and their life destroyed. Perhaps that is the reason, despite their depressing recent history, that the Keys have been the site for a remarkable number of successful conservation efforts. One of the first was the drive around the turn of the century to establish adequate protection for the bird life of the nation. At that time, as is true today, certain women's fashions required the destruction of wild nature. Today it is the skins of rare mammals that some female socialites insist upon wearing, despite the fact that they thus condemn to suffering and ultimate extinction the species involved. In the 1900s, it was the plumage of rare birds. The herons, egrets, spoonbills, ibises, and other plume-bearing species of the Everglades and the Keys were being pushed to the point of extinction by plume hunters. Although protective laws were on the books, these were virtually meaningless when there were no law-enforcement personnel in the field.

It was fitting that the newly created Audubon Society should get into this battle, since it was at Key West that Audubon had once found a home. With private funds, the society employed wardens to guard the bird rookeries of the glades and the Keys. One of their first wardens, Guy Bradley, who met his death in a gun battle with poachers near Flamingo, became a martyr to the conservation cause. As a result, the movement toward bird conservation gained strength, and the federal and state governments began to assume their proper roles in wildlife law enforcement. It was the Audubon Society, however, that placed a warden to protect with great success the breeding ground of the roseate spoonbill. Spreading out from Bottlepoint Key, the spoonbills, by 1963, were nesting on 10 different keys, and by 1970, were to be seen over much of their former range. Robert Porter Allen of National Audubon did much to bring about this increase by directing, through his writing, national interest toward these birds. His place, in Tavernier, has subsequently been taken by Sandy Sprunt (Alexander Sprunt, IV) who brings to his job the same enthusiasm and spirit that seem to characterize all the Audubon professionals. His efforts have been concentrated on the flamingos, brown pelicans, and white-crowned pigeons.

One of the great conservation successes for the Keys was the establishment of Everglades National Park in 1948. This brought under federal ownership and protection all the smaller keys north from Largo and the Matecumbes in

Florida Bay. Unfortunately, through an unwillingness to interfere with the Intracoastal Waterway, Lignum Vitae Key, a unique area, was left outside the boundaries of the park and without protection. One of the owners of this key, who had lost his holdings on Cape Sable through condemnation and purchase by the national park, developed a sour attitude toward conservation. His attempts to have the county build a causeway to his key, thus enhancing its development values, were forestalled by the efforts of conservation groups and subsequently stopped by the intervention of Florida's governor. This evidently did little to improve his attitude since he has subsequently turned down an offer of over a million dollars for the purchase of the key by the Nature Conservancy.

The first federal wildlife refuge to be established on the Keys was created with little controversy. This was the Key West National Wildlife Refuge, established in 1908. It includes all the sandy keys westward from Key West up to and including the Marquesas. With the establishment of Everglades National Park, protection was also offered to the Dry Tortugas, which because of the presence of historic Fort Jefferson, qualified as a national monument. Thus all the islands west of Key West are now afforded some degree of federal protection. The Tortugas are not only a traditional breeding ground for sea turtles, but support great breeding colonies of sooty, noddy, and royal terns. They are a concentration spot for the incredibly graceful man-of-war bird and for great numbers of other sea birds. The white-crowned pigeon and other rare upland birds also occur in this area. Fortunately, status as part of the national wilderness system has now been provided for the

Marquesas, and it seems likely that this island region may remain relatively undisturbed.

The same cannot be said for the islands of the Great White Heron Refuge. This heron, which resembles the American egret but is the largest of American herons, suffered originally from plume hunters and other depredation. Then the 1935 hurricane struck across its home ground, and reduced its numbers to an estimated 146. Therefore, in 1938, the Great White Heron Refuge was established for its protection. With such aid the species has increased greatly and is no longer on the list of endangered species.

The refuge, however, which extends north of the highway from Key West to Bahia Honda Key and includes most of the outlying keys in this region, is impressive only on the map. Since many of the islands within it are privately owned, they will be subject to development in the future. Thus, in 1968, development of the Tarpon Belly Keys, in the heart of the refuge, was proposed. These were presumably to become an "ocean farm" to raise shrimp for the market, on the surface a laudable objective. In fact, however, everything about the proposed plans was directed toward future use by real-estate entrepreneurs. Since dredge-and-fill permits were required, the state and federal governments were brought into the picture. The state approved, but through the leadership of Jack Watson and Art Marshall of the Bureau of Sport Fisheries and Wildlife, federal approval was withheld and the proposal died, at least for the present. However, a proposed but completely unnecessary extension of the Intracoastal Waterway, right through the heart of the refuge, has been brought forth by the Army Corps of Engineers. Alternative routes that would avoid the refuge are readily available, but such would not open up lands for development. Such an extension would make conditions in the refuge very difficult. They are already bad enough. For instance, the task of patrolling this vast area of water, in addition to the Key Deer Refuge, falls to just one warden. Catching a law violator can be only a matter of good luck and the sub rosa cooperation of the general public.

The struggle over the key deer marked another major gain for conservation in the Keys. This deer is not as diminutive as it is sometimes described to be. An adult buck can weigh as much as 95 pounds, and a doe, up to 65 pounds, although the averages are less. It once ranged throughout the lower Keys, but as these were settled and developed, it was pushed back from its former range by a combination of overhunting and destruction of its habitat. In the 1940s, the deer lived only in the area from Little Pine to Cudjoe Key, with its metropolis on Big Pine Key. It is difficult to know how many survived, but in 1947, it was estimated that only 50 were left. Although they were protected by Florida law, this protection was more on paper than in reality.

In 1950, efforts to save the key deer were started. Jack Silver of the Fish and Wildlife Service and Ding Darling, the cartoonist and one-time head of the same organization, joined forces in a campaign to direct public attention toward the deer. Money was raised to put the present warden, Jack Watson, on the job for full-time protection of the deer. A temporary refuge was proclaimed by the Fish and Wildlife Service in 1954. However, congressional approval was essential before the refuge could become permanent and lands could be purchased by the government. Congressmen Dante Fascell from Monroe County and Charles Bennett of Jacksonville led the effort to get legislation passed. It was a slow process. Not until 1957 was the bill approved to establish the National Key Deer Refuge, and even then only $35,000 was appropriated for land purchase.

Fortunately, private interest was sufficiently aroused so that more funds became available. C. R. "Pink" Gutermuth of the Wildlife Management Institute and the North American Wildlife Foundation deserves maximum credit for directing and coordinating the attempt to raise money. The foundation raised $186,000 for land purchase, acquiring the 715 acres of Howe Key and 75 acres of Big Pine Key. The Audubon Society also raised $185,000 and purchased an additional 112 acres for the refuge. The Crane Foundation of Miami contributed much of the money involved. In 1963, the refuge was officially dedicated, and by 1965, included 6,745 acres, of which less than 1,000 acres was owned and the balance leased by the federal government. Under protection and with habitat management, including controlled burning to improve the quality of the forage, the number of key deer increased. In 1965, its numbers were estimated at 350. Interestingly enough, Jack Watson reports that with improved forage, the deer are increasing in size as well as in numbers. Whether or not they will have the same public appeal if they grow into big deer remains to be seen.

In general, conservation efforts in Florida have been directed more toward the land and its animal and plant life than toward the water. Only in recent years has it been realized that underwater environments are as unique and priceless as those above the sea. However, the great interest in skin diving and scuba diving has made people conscious of a world from which they had previously been cut off, or could at best view darkly through the glass bottom of a boat. Fortunately, Florida has taken a lead in underwater marine conservation, and the Keys have been the center for activity.

The main coral area of Florida is the reef extending from Miami to the Dry Tortugas, 260 miles long and averaging 4 miles in depth. Separating the Gulf Stream from the shallow waters of the bays and sounds, it includes a fantastic array of marine life, ranging from the various coral animals through the great varieties of shellfish and other invertebrates to hundreds of species of fish, including many of the most brightly colored and spectacularly marked species known. Although not rated as one of the truly great reef areas of the world by coral connoisseurs, it is still brilliant and varied enough to dazzle the average venturer equipped with face mask and goggles. Unfortunately, like most other great natural assets, it was being increasingly plundered, particularly after World War II. Unrestricted spearfishing, shell collecting, and even dynamiting of the reefs to obtain coral and shells were threats to its continued existence.

Interest in preserving undisturbed areas of the reef for scientific study and public enjoyment has grown in Florida since the 1940s. When Everglades National Park was being created, an interested group of Florida conservationists attempted to extend its boundaries to include the coral reef. However, this proved politically difficult at that time, and efforts were therefore directed toward the state legislature. Years passed, but in time the efforts bore fruit. In 1960, over two thousand acres of land on Key Largo and seventy-five square miles of reef and water off Key Largo were designated as a Florida state coral reef park. The park was named for the man who had done much to promote it, John Pennekamp of the *Miami Herald*. It remains the only state park of its kind in America. Public access to the reefs is provided by glass-bottomed boats, and for those who like to explore on their own, boat ramps, boat rentals, and diving equipment are available.

Efforts to preserve the coral-reef environment did not stop with the establishment of Pennekamp park. In the 1960s, the federal government came back into the act with plans to set aside the northern end of the Keys and coral reef in the area between Key Largo and Miami. After another long struggle, Biscayne National Monument was established by Congress in 1968 and is now, very slowly, being purchased by the federal government. (Congress likes to make broad proclamations but rarely likes to appropriate the cash needed to give them substance.) When complete, it will protect a wild area of water, mangroves, coral reef, and upland hammock vegetation centering on Elliott Key and Rhodes Key and adjacent to metropolitan Miami. The fight for this national monument was led and won in Congress by the same Dante Fascell who had spearheaded the effort to set aside the Key Deer Refuge.

I went out to what is now Biscayne National Monument just before Congress approved its creation, along with Frank Craighead and several national park rangers. Both the upland and marine environments were fascinating to see, but the difficulty that is encountered in such conservation struggles was well illustrated. Shortly before, one of the landowners on Elliott Key had bulldozed a wide strip from one end of the key to the other, right through the

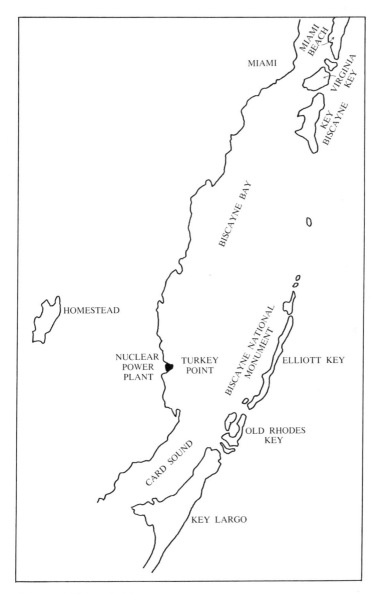

Biscayne National Monument.

To destroy the features that made the island worthy of protection a landowner cut a swath through the heart of the forests of Elliott Key.

middle of some of the best-developed and most fascinating tropical hammocks. Purely by accident, he missed eliminating the last-known wild stand of the rare Sargent's palm that remains anywhere on earth. In a way it was fortunate that Dade County had owned a county park on Elliott Key prior to this insult. The landowner had carelessly run his strip through part of the county park, and the county authorities were suing him for replacement costs on each of the trees and shrubs destroyed—at nursery prices. The bill for over a million dollars has set a good precedent, regardless of what the courts may decide.

Conservation battles are never completely won. Although the monument stands at Biscayne, the Florida Power and Light Company is constructing an atomic power plant just across the bay at Turkey Point. Such a plant, like all others, will produce great quantities of heated water as an effluent, in addition to the usual array of radio-active contaminants (admittedly at levels that the Atomic Energy Commission deems safe). The amount of water needed for cooling this plant, drawn from the already warm tropical waters of Biscayne Bay, would result in almost complete use of the waters of the southern bay for cooling, at periodic, brief intervals. Running these waters through the generators of the plant would of course destroy all the plankton and aquatic life that they contain. Water that is too warm to support life and that is depleted of existing life would then be returned to the bay. Of what value then would be the National Monument as a sanctuary for marine life? Fortunately, then Secretary of the Interior Walter Hickel saw fit to seek an injunction to halt further construction on the plant until such time as adequate cooling facilities are installed. How the court fight will turn out cannot be predicted, but meanwhile the power company is threatening southwest Florida with an imminent brown-out if completion of the plant is forestalled, and the Miami papers have growled that Hickel won all his favorable publicity as a conservationist at the expense of Florida development.

In retrospect, however, it would seem that the story of the Keys has been a long series of conservation victories. Strangely enough, these victories have taken place in Monroe County, noted for having the least progressive attitudes toward either land-use or conservation. The victories have brought no cheers from the county government, which has watched as most of its land went under federal or state control. It would seem to the county officials that they have already given enough land to the cause of conservation and that now they should be allowed to develop the rest. Indeed, this is almost true. But some tasks remain to be done.

Still remaining without protection is what is now a unique area—Lignum Vitae Key. Although only 280 acres in size, it now contains the last and best representation of the original Keys' forest. I first visited Lignum Vitae with Sandy Sprunt of National Audubon and John Milton of the Conservation Foundation in January, 1968, and subsequently wrote a report calling for its acquisition and preservation. The visit was memorable. Nowhere else in Florida can one find such a unique collection of old-growth tropical hardwoods. Here the lignum vitae tree (*Guaiacum sanctum*) grows in quantity, and some specimens have been estimated to be a thousand years old (admittedly on the basis of tree-ring counts which in the tropics are unreliable). This species is noted for its unusually dense, heavy, oily wood. Since this wood is much valued for special-purpose uses, it was cut out in most areas years ago. Here also are great numbers of gumbo-limbos, including one specimen suspected to be the largest in the United States. Mastic, poisonwood, fiddlewood, mahogany, black ironwood, strangler fig, and crabwood are only a few of the more than sixty-five species of trees and shrubs on the island.

On Lignum Vitae the white-crowned pigeons come to feed on pigeon plum, hog plum, sea grape, and other fruits in what is probably one of the largest breeding populations left in the Keys. Here is to be found what Edward Wilson and Thomas Eisner, Harvard biologists, believe to be an invertebrate fauna, including rare and beautiful tree snails, that is representative of the primeval fauna of hardwood hammocks. In their words, "To enter the forest on Lignumvitae Key is to step far into the past, and to come as close as we ever will to witnessing the Keys as they were before the coming of man." These conditions result in part from the elevation of the key; much of the land is sixteen feet or more above mean sea level and consequently has been above the hurricane tides of the more recent storms. In part also, they result from the protection provided by the owners of the key who have kept the forest undisturbed. Unfortunately the area is in danger of imminent development. If ever the federal and state governments had a duty and obligation, it is to purchase and preserve this key before it is too late. It is unjust to ask private groups, such as the Nature Conservancy, to do the job when the public obligation is so obvious.

Lignum Vitae Key and Vicinity.

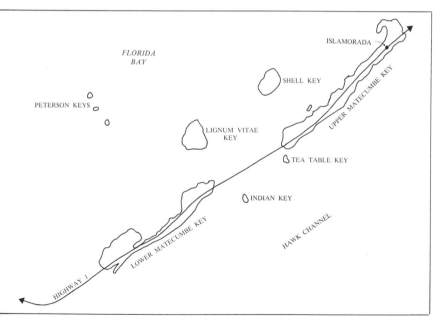

Lignum Vitae forms the apex of a triangle whose base rests on two other keys of great historical interest. One of these, Indian Key, was the site of the famous massacre when Chief Chekika led his band of Seminoles and Calusa survivors in an attack on the establishment of the wrecker Jacob Housman. In the killing died Dr. Henry Perrine, a benefactor of Florida agriculture who was the first to introduce and acclimatize many of the tropical crops now grown in the state. Near Indian Key is Tea Table Key where the U.S. Navy slept peacefully while the massacre was going on. Nobody would suggest that these two keys should be preserved for their natural values, but their historical interest is so great that they should receive attention as state or national monuments. The novels *Fort Everglades,* which describes Chekika's raid, and *A Journey to Matecumbe* have focused on the drama inherent in the events centering around the Matecumbe Keys and their outliers—Tea Table, Indian, and Lignum Vitae.

Out beyond Matecumbe, the obligation for conservation is fairly simple—purchase or otherwise secure those keys needed for the preservation of the Key Deer and Great White Heron refuges. Already the developers are eating into part of the Key Deer Refuge with major tracts growing up on Big Pine Key and a new road and causeway opening No Name Key to all comers. It is vital also to set aside a representative area of north Key Largo, with its distinctive animal and plant life, for future study and recreation. Key Largo is developing at a rate too rapid to permit further delay. Beyond these moves, however, conservation in the sense of preservation of wildlife and natural areas should probably rest on its accomplishments in the Florida Keys. This does not mean, however, that an interest in the environment of the Keys would therefore be satisfied. Monroe County has lagged inexcusably in its attention to zoning and planning. Development goes on without benefit of imagination or control.

The Florida Keys are a glorious place for people to live, and nobody in his right mind would want them set aside exclusively for wildlife. Provided that adequate safeguards are taken to protect against hurricane damage (little is being done now), the Keys could be one of America's most prized residential and recreational areas. Instead, they are a jumble of trailer camps, shacks, trash and debris, fly-by-night tourist-oriented enterprises, and general environmental chaos. They are badly in need of development so that people can live there. They are in need of proper development so that people can live there in dignity and enjoy their tropical environment. The county authorities

There is still an opportunity to develop the unique qualities of the Keys as a home for people.

have thus far been badly remiss in providing the leadership that the Keys so badly need. Controlled up to now by the Key West voters, the county commission has been oriented toward the urban problems of that city and inclined to approve anything in the outside area that would bring money to the county treasury. The result has been bad for Key West and disastrous for the other islands. Key West is a city of great historical interests. It is still one of the three or four most outstanding Florida communities. It could remain that way, preserving its historic past, and go forward to develop a new and fascinating city, oriented toward its environment and its potential role as a gateway to the Caribbean. It could incorporate all that is good in modern life and blaze a trail that other Caribbean countries would want to follow. The other keys could well develop that blend of natural environment and man-made amenity that would make them a mecca for planners and a center of national attention. But unless Monroe County's voters and the people of the state of Florida suffer a change of heart, this will not take place. This could be Florida's greatest tragedy.

Sanibel Beach

8 : To Speak of Other Islands

DURING THE SUMMER of 1968, I was provided with two months in Florida, by the Conservation Foundation, to do the writing that would result in this book. As usual, however, events overtook me, and I spent most of my time on our Rookery Bay project, in Florida biopolitics, and other more routine activities, and practically no time in writing. But it was a nice thought on the part of Russell Train, who was then my president. During these two months, I managed to put in an appearance at Hobe Sound where I was taken in tow by Nat Reed and shown the environs and its conservation problems.

Over the past few years, it has been difficult to talk about conservation in Florida without talking about Nathaniel P. Reed. After the election of Claude Kirk as governor in

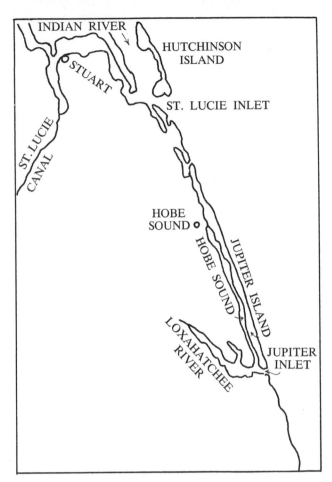

Jupiter Island and Vicinity.

1968, he was appointed conservation adviser and special assistant to the governor. Since he has developed both a good grasp of ecology and an understanding of human nature, he has been able to make remarkable progress in conservation matters, more than in any previous few years of state governmental activity.

Hobe Sound is the gateway to Jupiter Island, an area of Florida over which the Reed family has considerable influence. This island is not only of historical and biological interest, it also contains seasonally one of the great concentrations of wealth and power in North America. The result has been of ecological interest.

During my stay on Jupiter Island, I engaged in far more concentrated activity than I am accustomed to—skin diving to test the availability of lobsters on the Atlantic beach side, more skin diving to explore the depths of a warm lagoon, dense with algae, that Nat Reed was developing as a fish production area on the island, a tour by boat to look over the problems of Jupiter Inlet and the St. Lucie Canal with particular emphasis on beach erosion and turtle nesting, and finally a trip up the Loxahatchee River, one of the few wild rivers that remain in Florida. I realized that Nat Reed's success in Florida conservation was at least in part a result of an incredible amount of personal energy.

Jupiter Island is one of those environmentally superb areas that wealth can create when it is applied with imagination to an area of existing natural beauty. Because its inhabitants like what they have built and do not want it to be swamped by development encroaching from the outside, they have expended millions of dollars towards its protection. The north and south ends of the island have been purchased and turned over as natural sanctuaries to the Audubon Society and the Nature Conservancy. The area across Hobe Sound from the island that was not already included in the Jonathan Dickinson State Park was also purchased and set aside as a natural reserve. Except for the beach erosion that is eating away its shoreline, Jupiter Island has been rendered relatively secure. At least it will probably not be destroyed by the general environmental degradation that so often accompanies Florida development. Jupiter Island thus represents one approach to conservation, not to be ignored although not generally applicable—the encouragement of the wealthy to protect in their own way those environments that they deem desirable. Having saved many areas around the United States, this method is particularly efficacious when applied to island property.

Our egalitarian philosophy today leads those in authority to frown on enclaves of wealth and privilege. But if one is interested in maintaining environmental diversity and holding open the greatest opportunity for human diversity to develop, then private capital is an essential ally, complementing governmental activity. Government must play a major role in conservation, but there is no doubt that it is heavy-handed and has a tendency to grind toward a "lowest common denominator." Private wealth can accomplish miracles towards preserving the rare and otherwise unattainable, the emeralds and rubies of the natural world.

There is little that is environmentally unique about Jupiter. There are the long, wild beaches where the loggerheads roll up to breed each summer and some stretches of natural vegetation, but then there is too much invading casuarina. There are great schools of fish offshore and great numbers and varieties of birds. It has become to a degree unique because most other areas like it have been destroyed. Somewhere near here Ponce de León came ashore. Here Jonathan Dickinson landed after his shipwreck and experienced his nerve-wracking encounters with the Indians before making his way back north to the Yankee settlements. The original scene that he must have observed is today maintained only in the lower stretches of the palm-and-cypress–lined Loxahatchee River. However, it is the mix of man and nature, which shows what people can accomplish, that is most worthwhile on Jupiter Island.

A long way from Hobe Sound, way up on the Florida

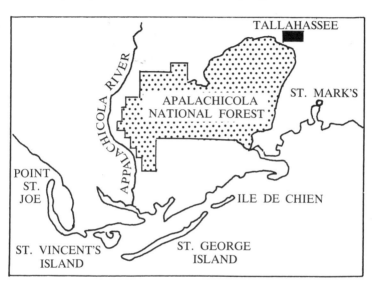

St. Vincent's Island and Vicinity.

panhandle, is St. Vincent's Island. Far back in the past this must have been a truly incredible island with its old pine forests, palm groves, and mix of other ancient woodland types. But human activity was not kind to it. At the end of World War II, St. Vincent's was in deplorable condition. The previous owners had "high-graded" the old slash-pine forests, taking whatever timber was valuable and leaving the debris. The wildlife had been poached into near extinction by hunters from the mainland. It was on the usual Florida skids down the long grade to nowhere. At that time, however, the Loomis brothers took it over and began to protect it. They were island people by preference who appreciated the solitude and natural beauty that St. Vincent's could provide. They could afford to hire men to patrol the beaches and keep intruders away. The idea of having an undisturbed beach—11 miles of broad white sand, fringed with pines and palms and fronting on the blue Gulf water —for the use of their family and friends was to them worth the high costs involved. Under their care over the past 20 years, the island has recovered from past misuse. The forests came back and the wildlife returned. When I came to St. Vincent's in 1967, with Henry Loomis, I was overwhelmed.

Canoeing down its undisturbed streams, watching alligators and herons, walking or riding at night down the long beach looking for loggerheads (over 50 had come ashore to breed that summer, and the summer was not over), exploring the marshes and woodlands, all added up to an unforgettable experience.

The dominant vegetation of St. Vincent's is slash-pine forest in which some longleaf pine is mixed. We visited some old groves of slash pine, isolated by marshes and consequently left alone by the loggers. Wood storks were roosting in the ancient pines, and one could imagine there how the island had once been, and some day may become again. There are also mixed hardwood forests with evergreen and deciduous oak, magnolia, tupelo gum, maple, and bay. There is an area of sand-pine scrub, undisturbed by logging and similar to that which occurs to the east in the Ocala forest. In one place is a great extent of cabbage-palm woodland in which the tall, straight palms are mixed with some equally tall and straight cedars. But most of the island supports marsh—fresh, salt, and brackish—which in turn supports the full spectrum of Florida marsh birds and provides

Canoe down streams through scenes of incredible beauty.

St. Vincent's, 11 miles of white beach fringed with palms and pines.

a home for the migratory ducks that pour in by the thousands in the winter. There are fresh-water lakes and streams not yet invaded by water hyacinth but covered by the native water lilies. White-tailed deer, wild turkeys, and bobwhite quail are everywhere. Ospreys and bald eagles still find a home on St. Vincent's.

My visit was the last to be paid to the island while it was under Loomis ownership. Circumstances had forced them to sell. Fortunately the federal government was able to move in and acquire St. Vincent's as part of the national wildlife refuge system. The Smithsonian Institution plans to establish a research station there. The island will change from what it has been, but its natural beauty and wild animal life should remain secure.

Old pines survived together with tall cabbage palms.

The owners of St. Vincent's had, over many decades, a taste for exotic animals. Back in 1905, sambar deer from India were introduced there. Quickly adapting to the swamps and marshes, they managed to survive the era of poaching. In 1967, they were almost as abundant as the native whitetails and considerably more spectacular. Wild hogs had also been introduced, growing into abundant and formidable animals. Cattle, once domestic, had run wild on the island. The Loomis brothers, however, went further than the previous owners. They brought in zebra and eland from Africa and black buck from India. It was incredible to encounter these creatures in a Florida environment, acting at home and at ease, when I had last seen them in the wild only on the dry plains of central Africa. But they seemed to be thriving. One eland bull had escaped to the mainland, swimming across the narrow strait. There it was encountered and shot by hunters who had no idea what strange animal they had bagged.

It might have been an interesting experiment if these exotic animals could have been studied over the years as they adjusted to a Florida island. Unfortunately, the federal government did not encourage such an investigation. The eland, zebra, and black buck had to go. The sambar and wild hogs will be much more difficult to eliminate. But St. Vincent's, for the most part, will support only its original native animal life.

Down where the Peace River and Myakka join with the Caloosahatchee in pouring their waters into Charlotte Harbor, Pine Island Sound, and San Carlos Bay, are the islands of Sanibel and Captiva. They are part of the barrier chain of islands that rings the mouth of these harbors. Sanibel is the larger, approximately twelve miles long by

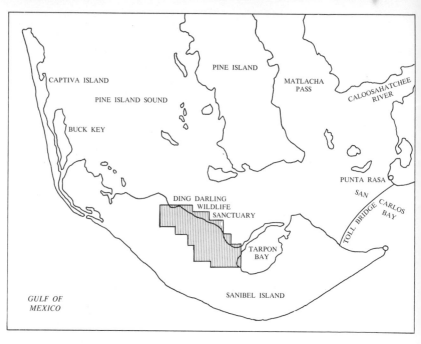

Sanibel and Captiva.

two miles wide. It is separated from the smaller Captiva Island by the narrow channel of Blind Pass, across which a highway bridge connects the two. Part of the complex is Buck Key, fronting on Blind Pass and separated from Captiva only by the narrow, mangrove-lined Roosevelt Channel. These islands are not the preserves of the very wealthy who could afford to purchase them in their entirety and maintain them virtually intact. They are, however, the home of a number of people of varying financial qualifications who had moved there because they were islands and because they were different. Over the years they had built up their own way of life and had hoped to be left alone.

Sanibel and Captiva have a long history, having been settled long before most of the towns on the Florida mainland. They have an even longer record in Florida legend as bases for piracy. Captiva is said to have gained its name from its service to the pirate Black Caesar, as a holding pen, so to speak, for his more beautiful female captives. The facts are somewhat different, but such a myth will always endure when history has been forgotten. On the Gulf side, the islands present a continuous front of broad sandy beach—shell sand, formed from the vast array of marine shells that are washed in from the Gulf and have played a major role in the formation of the islands.

The shell beaches of Sanibel–Captiva are known throughout the world. Here some four hundred varieties of shells have been identified, among them endangered forms of angel wing, horse conch, and king's crown. Countless numbers and colors of coquinas and cockles, whelks, clams, oysters, penshells, and cones are to be found. Fortunate shell hunters have been known to find the rare and highly valued Junonia, one of the volute shells. I can never resist coming home from Sanibel with a pocketful of shells, even though I am not really a collector and have no place for them. But that is the way they affect most people.

The bay side of Sanibel and Captiva is built up from mud and silt trapped by mangroves. In the interior is high ground that once supported dense hammock woodland and a fresh-water slough beneath which rests the island's fresh-water supply—a lens of water accumulated from past rainfall and at one time the sole source of drinking or irrigation water for the people.

Second only to the shell beaches, the bird life of Sanibel–Captiva attracts widespread attention. Nearly two hundred and fifty species have been recorded living in the islands. These include great numbers of migrants, for the islands are a resting and wintering ground on the Atlantic Flyway. Among the wintering ducks, the gadwall, pintail, blue-winged teal, widgeon, lesser scaup, and red-breasted merganser are common. The Florida duck breeds there in large numbers. Shovelers, redheads, canvasbacks, ring-necked ducks, and green-winged teal are sometimes present. Wading and sea birds are in abundance. I saw my first reddish egret and yellow-crowned night heron on Sanibel along with numbers of roseate spoonbills, wood storks, and the more common herons. West Indian species of upland birds are occasionally seen in addition to the greater range of more normal Florida residents and migrants.

In January, 1970, while exploring around the center of Sanibel, I was impressed by great numbers of tree swallows, wheeling in large flocks high in the air. I am not a good swallow-estimator, but I would guess that their numbers were in the tens of thousands. A cold snap had recently hit the area, killing off tarpon and horseshoe crabs in the shallow waters and suppressing the insect populations. This may explain the unusual maneuvers in which the swallows engaged. Wheeling in from all directions, the birds would descend in a concentrated mass, seemingly at times with only inches separating the rapidly flying individuals. On several occasions these great flocks descended almost upon me, circling and twisting within a few feet of my head. Their goal appeared to be to land momentarily on the shrubs and low trees, some clinging to their branches while keeping up their rapid wing beats and others flying in densely packed masses near the foliage. I assume the object was to stir up the quiescent insects, forcing them to fly so that they could be captured and eaten. After a few moments of this activity, the flocks would ascend once more and soon would be scattered in all directions over the island. Then, as if on signal, they would concentrate and

138

descend in another place, on some occasions landing on the ground or in the grass, but more commonly on trees and shrubs.

Never before have I been in the midst of such a closely packed mass of flying birds and must compare the experience with a scene from Alfred Hitchcock's movie *The Birds,* although the element of fear was absent. How these intricate maneuvers were organized, how the signals were given to concentrate and descend and then to ascend and scatter, and how so many densely packed birds could avoid collision, I must leave to the bird behaviorists or to God to answer. I can only record a certain awe that I reserve for fantastic natural phenomena.

Although Sanibel was used as a base almost from Spanish days, permanent settlement did not begin until the late nineteenth century, in the 1880s. Sanibel Light, a historic building on the island, was first erected in 1885. In 1888, the first resort hotel, which is still in existence, was opened on the island (the Casa Ybel). Agricultural efforts received the attention of the early settlers, but the occurrence of hurricanes at not infrequent intervals caused setbacks to this endeavor. A major hurricane in 1926 essentially eliminated farming from the island.

Several factors operated to prevent settlement—the distance from the mainland, only three miles but adequate to rule out those who don't like islands or boats; the scarcity of good drinking water; and the presence of mosquitoes. Mosquitoes are everywhere in Florida, but Sanibel had an unusual claim to fame. Maurice Provost, director of the Entomological Research Center of the Florida State Board of Health, at Vero Beach, records that a single light trap set under a sea grape near the ferry landing, in 1950, caught a total of 365,696 mosquitoes in a single night, which claims a world record. He found mosquito-egg densities in Sanibel Slough as high as 45,000 per square foot and states that swales on Sanibel holding half a billion eggs per acre was common. There is no doubt that mosquitoes discouraged all but the most hardy and resistant visitors and settlers.

An account of Sanibel written in the late 1930s gives its population at 100 people, of whom 10 were concentrated in the town of Wulfert, on the northern end near Blind Pass "surrounded by a dense tropical jungle in which towering coconut palms predominate." Captiva had a total of 45 inhabitants. But after World War II, despite the mosquitoes, people who were attracted by the islands began to move there. Fortunately there was no massive real-estate development. Most came as individuals, building their own kinds of houses in ways that did little damage to the total landscape. But then came mosquito control.

Thanks to the ability of Maurice Provost and his associates, mosquitoes were controlled with a minimal use of pesticides. In their place, Provost used water management and fresh-water fish. By a canal system and water-control structures, it was possible to hold fresh water supporting great numbers of topminnows and killifish (both voracious feeders on mosquito larvae) in areas in which water levels previously had fluctuated with the tides and which often supported few predators on mosquitoes. Since the salt-marsh mosquito lays eggs on moist soil and depends on seasonal flooding by rainwater or tidal flow for hatching and the growth of larvae, the system of control used by Provost worked admirably. There are still mosquitoes on the island, but they are no longer sufficiently abundant to cause much concern.

By the end of 1964, those who didn't like island isolation had removed two other barriers to island settlement. Fresh water had been piped to the island, and a causeway connecting Sanibel to the mainland near the old seaport town of Punta Rassa had been completed. The proposed causeway had been fought desperately by the islanders who feared an influx of developers and tourists, but they lost. At best, they managed to charge a three-dollar bridge toll for entrance to the island; the exit has no toll. However the old way of life seemed at an end. Extensive land clearing, dredging and filling, and canal building began to clear the way for tract houses and a burgeoning growth of motels.

Neither Sanibel nor Captiva are suited, in their totality, to be natural reserves. They were settled too long ago and changed too drastically over much of their area to qualify. Much of the vegetation is now exotic, and the Australian casuarina dominates in place of the old hammock forests. However, there is enough of a mix of the natural and man-made to be pleasant, and on the mangrove side of the islands, things are little changed from presettlement days.

The outlook for maintaining the present island environment is not all dark. From even the early days the islands have been known to conservationists. Teddy Roosevelt caught a giant manta ray off Captiva on one of his many deep-sea fishing excursions to this area and knew the islands well. J. N. "Ding" Darling began to visit Sanibel in the days before he became chief of the U.S. Biological Survey (now the Bureau of Sport Fisheries and Wildlife). He was instrumental in having the islands declared a state game reserve. More effective protection and management came when acquisition of lands around Tarpon Bay on the mangrove side of the island was approved by the Migratory

Bird Conservation Committee in 1943, with a view to the establishment of a national wildlife refuge. In 1947, President Truman extended federal protection to migratory birds on all of Sanibel, the southern end of Captiva, and surrounding water areas. In 1967, a refuge named the Ding Darling National Wildlife Refuge came into being, including over 600 acres of federal land and 1,900 acres leased from the state of Florida. When fully purchased, or otherwise acquired, the refuge will take in 800 acres of brackish water impoundments, 1,000 acres of bay water, 100 acres of fresh-water marsh and impoundments, 10 acres of beach, 500 acres of wooded uplands, and 2,300 acres of mangrove swamp.

The fight to protect Sanibel, however, was not led by the federal government, but by the local citizens. They deserve most of the credit for the federal accomplishment. Organized into the Sanibel–Captiva Conservation Foundation, they continue to strive to maintain their local environment. Their goals are reasonable. They seek to maintain the fresh-water marsh as a means for keeping a stable system of fresh water on the island and to acquire the necessary land to round out the federal refuge. Beyond that, they seek to control development, keeping it to the uplands, to avoid the disruption of aquatic life that would result from dredging and filling. They wish most of all to avoid the standardized, Florida-style proliferation of the ordinary at the expense of the irreplaceable. But achieving these modest aims seems to require continuous, all-out warfare against those who seek only to maximize their personal profits.

Weed-Choked Waterway

9 : The Great Barge Boondoggle

IT ALL STARTED with worry about pirates and the fact that
the coral reefs off the Florida Keys were sending far too
many sailing ships to the bottom. Andrew Jackson was
President, and Commodore Porter had yet to lead his Key
West squadron into their final and conclusive antipiracy
actions. Florida was viewed primarily as an impediment to
navigation between the mouth of the Mississippi and the
eastern coast of the United States and as a refuge for riff-
raff. In itself, it was considered to be of little or no economic importance. And so the shipowners dreamed of
somehow isolating Florida from the rest of the nation by
cutting a ship canal across its northern limits. Their message came through to government, and an idea that was to
be as persistent as the common cold took root in Washington.

In time, such a passage across Florida was indeed constructed. One of Florida's early entrepreneurs, Hamilton
Disston, purchased from a bankrupt state government, at
the cost of 25 cents an acre, a total of 4 million acres of
what was called swamp-and-overflow land—wetlands inherited by Florida from the federal government. In his little
empire Disston engaged his passion for canal building, hop-
ing to tie his capital, Kissimmee, to the Gulf of Mexico and
develop it into a great transportation center. Starting in
1881, he dredged the Kissimmee River, Lake Okeechobee,
and the Caloosahatchee River so that boats of shallow draft
could be brought from the Mississippi to the middle of
Florida. But railway expansion was already in full swing,
and the railroads soon knocked Disston's canal network
out of commercial operation. Nevertheless, the route up
the Caloosahatchee remained important to the new settlements on the west coast and to the agricultural areas that
were springing up around Lake Okeechobee. In 1909, in
an effort to benefit the local economy and to pursue the old
dream of a cross-Florida canal, Congress appropriated
money to "improve" the Caloosahatchee River and construct a waterway down the old St. Lucie River to connect
Fort Myers on the Gulf with Fort Lauderdale on the Atlantic.

In 1912, the first steamboats could cross Florida, safe
from pirates and coral reefs. But, of course, the pirates had
long since gone and safe passage beyond the coral reefs was
now taken for granted. Railroads dominated the national
transportation picture. Still, this early canal was of some
value, and its damage to the local environment was not
noticeable. Florence Fritz has described a voyage of the
first steamboat, the *Suwannee*: "She steamed slowly so that

passengers might observe the exciting tropical vegetation which sometimes met across the narrow jungle stream. Palms, moss-hung oaks, isolated homesteads, steamer-landings of settlers came into view and were passed. There were wild birds; and alligators sunned on the banks. Deer occasionally came down to drink. Far beyond was the mysterious land of the everglades." A similar description might have been written of another steamboat ride on another Florida river at that time—the ride up the Oklawaha River to Silver Springs. But, of course, such an idyllic scene could not be left alone.

By the 1960s, the Okeechobee Waterway, as it was then called, was under the jurisdiction of the Army Corps of Engineers. In 1962, 304,391 tons of shipping passed through it. In 1961, with a $42 million appropriation, and working together with the Central and South Florida Flood Control District, the Corps of Engineers started a program to enlarge the Caloosahatchee from 90 feet to a 180- to 225-foot width and to increase its depth from 8 feet to 24 feet. The old tropical verdure and trees overhanging the narrow stream were necessarily to go. The steamboat trip was to become a thing of the past. Flood control was joined to navigation to guarantee that water could move down the Caloosahatchee and the St. Lucie with the greatest of speed and with minimum impediment. Later, the Kissimmee River, draining into Lake Okeechobee, was to be further dredged and straightened to guarantee that waters would flow into Okeechobee faster than the enlarged Okeechobee Waterway could drain them out, and thus threaten new floods. But that is another story.

In the 1930s, there were few defenders of the Florida environment and no real shortage of wilderness in Florida.

The city of Miami had a population somewhat in excess of 110,000. On the west coast, Naples was a thriving town of 390 people. Jacksonville, then the state's largest city, bulged with somewhat less than 130,000. Tampa, the metropolis of the west, mustered somewhat over 101,000 inhabitants. But a high proportion of all these people were out of work and on relief.

A great make-work scheme was called for, and as ever there were people around with ideas of how federal money could best be spent. It might be thought that with the Okeechobee Waterway in operation, the advocates of a cross-Florida canal would have become quiescent, but this was not so. It seemed that many shippers, shipowners, bargemen, and waterway advocates lived in the past, having never recovered from the great days of the Erie Canal. And so the plans for the cross-Florida ship canal were brought out once more. The canal would cut across northern Florida, starting in the vicinity of Yankeetown on the Gulf. It would move up the winding, scenic channels of the Withlacoochee River, then cut through the limestone backbone of Florida to connect on the east with the Oklawaha River and move through its dark, cypress-filled wilderness to the broad reaches of the St. Johns. From there it would be easy travel to Jacksonville and the Atlantic. Such a scheme, advanced by Florida's congressmen, captured the imagination of the United States Congress. Five million dollars were appropriated.

In 1935, men and mules went to work. They worked surprisingly fast and did an impressive job. In 1970, it can all be seen clearly from the air. Soil and vegetation have been removed from Yankeetown inland in a broad swath over rights-of-way that were acquired for very little cash.

For only one year did they work, but the damage done has been beyond the capacity of nature to repair in 35 years.

If the ship canal had been constructed, it would have been at sea level. Biting deep into the Floridian aquifer, it would have brought salt water from the Gulf and the Atlantic into the limestone rock that carries water supplies all the way south to Everglades City. Such a simple, but apparently not obvious, truth had to be pointed out by the Geological Survey after work on the ship canal had already started. This threat to Florida's water supply, in combination with various political factors, caused the ship canal to be abandoned in 1936. The canal advocates had been put down, but they were not closed out. With a ship canal out of the picture, they shifted over to the idea of a barge canal, with locks and barriers to salt-water intrusion, that would not cut so deeply into the Floridian aquifer, biting only a short distance into the highly porous, indeed cavernous, Ocala limestone formation.

World War II arrived, and German submarines sank Allied shipping in the south Atlantic, the Caribbean, and the Gulf. The canal advocates came to life. If only we had the canal, they said, all that tonnage and all those lives might have been saved. The boats and barges could move quietly across a fully protected waterway. Congress was swayed and in 1942 authorized the construction of the canal. The War Department, however, was not swayed, stating flatly that the canal could contribute little to the war effort. Nevertheless, the Corps of Engineers were brought back into the picture.

There is nothing intrinsically wrong with the Army Corps of Engineers. They are good engineers, and they are noted for doing their job on time. But for reasons peculiar to our political history, they are the great "pork barrel" agency of our government. Congressmen who want federal money and federally supported jobs brought into their districts come out strongly for army corps projects. Other congressmen, waiting for their turns at the federal faucet, rarely object. The corps is thus the tool of all those who wish to share the wealth that is to be squeezed from the taxpayer, and it is a most effective tool. There is no reason why the corps should not be doing worthwhile things for the nation. They have no inherent objection to doing so. But in fact they have become involved with many of the most environmentally destructive projects in the United States. Once they are involved, they are hard to beat, since they are devoted to their objectives and pursue them with a persistence and single-mindedness that their opponents seldom have the time or the capability to turn aside. So it was to be with the Cross-Florida Barge Canal.

Viewing the project from its engineering problems and considering only a narrow range of economic costs, the corps decided that the route of the old ship canal, with some minor modifications, was the most feasible route for the barge canal. It was not, however, until 1958 that pressure to build the canal was seriously renewed by Florida's legislators. In that year the corps presented "An Economic Restudy of the Cross-Florida Barge Canal." The pressure continued to build. In 1962, in fulfillment of his campaign promises, President Kennedy went before Congress to ask for funds to start work, once again, on the long-abandoned canal. Congress, of course, was amenable. The work started, and the chain of events that led to the crisis which was to come was set in motion.

The year 1962 had little in common with 1942, 1935, or 1820. In a world in which submarines were used primarily to transport atomic weapons, the defense value of a barge canal was not only trivial but negative. Today, the Department of Defense has already rejected it. The need for barge canals in a world of superhighways, supertankers, pipe lines, and the old reliable railroads has dwindled enormously from what existed in the past. In fact, those who would have benefited from a canal as a means for transportation were few indeed. They were so few that the value of cheap transportation was inadequate in the Corps' cost–benefit analysis when weighed against the cost of the canal. But knowing, or presuming that they knew, on which side their political bread was buttered, the corps brought out its usual range of "side benefits" to be added to the transportation benefit that the canal was to produce.

By some magic, the canal and its impoundments were to become recreationally attractive. It was to enhance the value of all lands along or near its route. It was to bring great benefits to Florida's economy and encourage healthy regional growth. By these calculations, and by boosting the volume of traffic that the canal might someday carry (twenty-first-century barge traffic was assumed to be remarkably heavy), the benefits of the canal were made to exceed by a minute margin the estimated costs. Aiding these calculations was a tendency to continue discount rates or interest rates that were appropriate to the late 1950s into the 1970s and beyond, in the hope that this would be ignored by the Bureau of the Budget (as indeed it was).

In the 1960s, however, other facts about Florida had also changed. No longer was it a wilderness state. The spread of urbanization and transportation networks, of farms and pastures and closely managed plantation forests, had imposed a checkerboard pattern of human handiwork

CROSS-FLORIDA BARGE CANAL

ST. AUGUSTINE

DAYTONA BEACH

LAKE GEORGE

ST. JOHNS LOCK
RODMAN DAM

ST. JOHNS RIVER

PALATKA

OKLAWAHA RIVER

OCALA NATIONAL FOREST

GAINESVILLE

EUREKA DAM

SILVER SPRINGS

OCALA

BERT DOSH LOCK

DUNNELLON

DUNNELLON LOCK

YANKEETOWN

INGLIS

INGLIS LOCK

SUWANEE RIVER

CEDAR KEYS

COMPLETED PORTION

over the once unconfined wild land. The area available for natural vegetation, for wildlife, for any possibility of human recreation away from the urban crowds, had shrunk to a minimum size. The Everglades and the Ten Thousand Islands, far to the south, retained the qualities of wilderness. A small stretch along the Loxahatchee retained some wild river characteristics. Beyond these, there was the Suwannee and the northern Gulf Coast from Apalachee Bay to Cedar Keys which remained tolerably wild (construction of the Intracoastal Waterway link southward from St. Marks to hook up with the barge canal would change this also). Finally, there was the wild Oklawaha River valley. Wilderness and wild country of any kind had become a scarce, almost priceless, commodity.

As funds for the barge canal became available and the big machines were moved into position, those who could see the value of wilderness attempted to obtain a hearing. The Friends of the Oklawaha came into existence, based in Gainesville and led by Marjorie Carr, the biologist wife of Dr. Archie Carr, and by David Anthony, a biochemist at the University of Florida.

But the time was not yet right. The words *environment* and *ecology* were still little known among the general public. Pollution was known, but was still regarded only as an untidy byproduct of the great American march into a future to be made golden by technology. The earth-moving machines began to roll, the dredges started to scoop up the deep, organic soils, and a giant crusher, devised for the purpose, rolled over the rich forests of the Oklawaha flood plain, crushing the life of the land down deep into the muck.

Up from Yankeetown, following the old ship-canal

route, the new barge canal cut through the meanders of the Withlacoochee, smashing down its palms and cypresses to form a barren channel up to Dunnellon and beyond. Dams and locks were built, and new reservoirs came into being. On the east the Oklawaha suffered as the engineers moved up from the Saint Johns at Palatka to build a great dam at Rodman and halt the flow of the river. Then they moved on to start completion of another dam at Eureka, not far downstream from where the crystal waters of Silver Springs Run drain into the Oklawaha.

But the Oklawaha was not just another river. It was the life line of a flood-plain wilderness forest, the haunt of unique and spectacular wildlife, one of the last homes of the panther and the black bear in Florida. Here were to be found species in greater number and variety—both plant and animal—of northern and tropical origin than could be identified in any comparable region of central or northern Florida. This was the very last of the old Florida of William Bartram and Audubon. After Rodman Pool had been completed and part of the Oklawaha had been destroyed, the value of the rest of it was at long last recognized. The Friends of the Oklawaha, having grown into a larger and stronger organization, the Florida Defenders of the Environment, rallied support from scientists and conservationists from around the nation. In 1969, with the help of the Environmental Defense Fund, they instituted a lawsuit against the corps to stop the canal. From an obscure place on the back pages of the Florida newspapers, the barge canal moved forward into the limelight of television. From the viewpoint of the canal advocates, the exposure was hardly welcome. By then, $50 million of federal money had been put into the ground, but a minimum of $100 million more was thought necessary to complete the canal, assuming that all went the way that the corps wanted it to go. The canal was one-third complete, but the vital two-thirds that included the major part of the Oklawaha River system had yet to be affected.

In late 1969, Florida conservation won its greatest battle of all in the defeat of the Everglades jetport. Success brings support and new hope. As 1970 started, the Florida Defenders of the Environment, led now by Bill Partington, on leave from the Florida Audubon Society and assisted ably by Marjorie Carr, began to realize that they might at long last win the barge-canal battle. Some of the strongest advocates of the canal, including Florida's secretary of state, found their ethics and motives under serious scrutiny in the press. People began to ask why it was that Florida's Department of Natural Resources contained so many former colonels from the Corps of Engineers. Florida's Department of Game and Fresh-water Fish issued a report condemning the canal. In a speech at Gainesville, Governor Kirk questioned the wisdom of proceeding with the canal. In Washington, Secretary of the Interior Hickel ordered a restudy of the canal by the Bureau of Sport Fisheries and Wildlife. Virtually every environmental scientist familiar with the region signed a letter to President Richard Nixon requesting a reconsideration of the canal. The problem was passed over to Russell Train, the newly appointed chairman of the federal Council on Environmental Quality, for disposal.

Meanwhile, the Florida Defenders of the Environment has issued its own report, prepared by a large number of independent, nongovernment scientists, that calls into question virtually every argument advanced in favor of the canal. The report spotlights the shaky economic justification of the waterway, the serious risks from pollution that could endanger the water supply in the Floridian aquifer, and the enormous ecological damage that would be done. The final results are not in. They can be vital to Florida and the nation. If those who favor development at any cost lose this battle, then the way may really be clear to save the American environment.*

* While this book was in press President Nixon followed the advice of his Council and ordered a halt to further construction of the barge canal.

Melaleuca

10 : Exotic Things

My first, but I hope not my last, experience with scuba diving took place in an unusual place—Florida's Ichetucknee River. (I regret that most of Florida's rivers are virtually unspellable and unpronounceable to a non-native, but the Indians who named them had no such difficulties.) If you don't already know where the Ichetucknee is, don't go looking for it. It is a small stream and can't stand much people-pressure. Nevertheless it is one of what once were many sparkling, clear streams that bubble up from limestone caverns in Florida and contribute their pristine waters to the lakes and major rivers of the state.

The Ichetucknee emerges from blue caverns whose deep chambers would tempt more adventurous divers than I, having indeed tempted some to disaster. I was led there by

Lyman Rogers, who put me into diving gear before I could begin to object, ran me through some safety maneuvers, and then sent me off downstream. From then on I managed on my own, staring face to face with fish who clearly did not believe in me, looking at the brilliant colors of water plants, and poking around the edges of the deep grottos from which the waters emerged. I found it necessary then to add another name to the list of places that must be

Fresh-Water Springs.

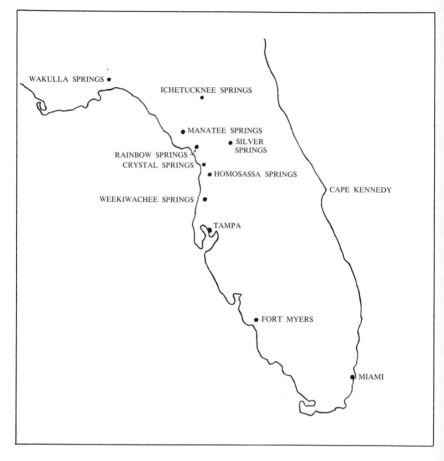

preserved at all costs. Fortunately, others agreed, and the Ichetucknee became in 1969 a new state park.

There are not now many limestone springs or streams that have not been developed for tourism or other uses, but the Ichetucknee is one. Still, the ones that have been developed are magnificent, even when viewed through the bottom of a glass-bottomed boat in the company of scores of fellow visitors. The Ichetucknee Springs are the third largest in Florida, pouring out a total of 340 cubic feet of water per second as an average rate of flow. The larger two are Silver Springs, with an output of 800 cubic feet per second, and Rainbow Springs, with 700. Both of these have been built up as tourist centers. Silver Springs, now the center of a resort community, is the oldest and in many ways most spectacular tourist attraction in Florida; here you can see incredible underwater panoramas and watch herds of sea fish mingle with fresh-water species in water that is too clear to be believed.

Today, however, the quality and clarity of all Florida's water is threatened. Pollution is a basic cause, but adding to this and deriving from it is the invasion by a great variety of exotic water weeds, all of which have proved well adapted to existence in the lakes, streams, estuaries, and springs of Florida. Thus the Crystal River, where forty to fifty of Florida's endangered manatees spend their winter months, was once a warm, pellucid stream. Now it is being choked with a growing mass of the Florida elodea (*Hydrilla verticillata*), one of Florida's most vigorous exotic invaders.

The exotic water plants usually enter Florida by apparently harmless means, brought in by dealers to supply people who wish to grow them in aquariums or use them as ornamental oxygen producers in a garden fish pond. But somehow people seem to tire of their aquariums or feel the need to clean out their ponds, so they dump or drain them into some local stream. Soon the exotic is off and away. Thus, Dick Pothier, writing in the *Miami Herald,* had described the arrival of the water hyacinth. It was first brought to the United States as an ornamental plant to be used in a display at the Japanese Pavilion during a New Orleans exposition in 1884. A visiting Floridian, attracted by the beautiful hyacinth blooms, brought some home for her fish pond. She then had the idea that the nearby St. Johns River would be beautified by the presence of some of these delightful purple blooms. The St. Johns was always rich in nutrients and in aquatic vegetation. Bartram described the great masses of the native water lettuce that grew on it during the eighteenth century. It was thus an ideal home for the hyacinth, which proceeded to take over. Unfortunately, not only the St. Johns but most of Florida's rivers and lakes provided a similarly ideal habitat. The water hyacinth is now almost ubiquitous.

Speaking objectively, hyacinths are beautiful, and few would complain about them were they not prolific beyond belief. It is said that in Florida, the offspring of 20 adult hyacinths will cover 20 acres of water surface in a single growing season. They form a complete carpet over the water surface, which rules out the use of the water for boating or swimming. In time they choke off channels and restrict water flow, thus becoming a major impairment of drainage canals and irrigation ditches. Upon dying, the hyacinths fall to the bottom and build up a dense layer of organic litter which restricts the water-holding capacity of ponds and reservoirs. Shading the surface of streams or lakes, they prevent sunlight from penetrating the water, making it impossible for underwater aquatic plants, which add oxygen to the water, to grow. When the hyacinths die and decay, they use what oxygen is already present in the water, thus creating conditions under which fish and other aquatic animals cannot live. To prevent these problems, Florida spends over a million dollars a year on hyacinth control. It has not been adequate. The hyacinths still thrive.

Although hyacinths can grow in relatively sterile environments, they thrive best in waters enriched by the addition of phosphates and nitrates through the processes of water pollution. Raw sewage, or the effluent of most existing sewage treatment plants and of septic tanks, and the runoff from fertilized farm lands and city gardens all add these nutrients to water. Thus the growth of aquatic plants is encouraged. The result is a process long known to ecologists, that of eutrophication. Eutrophication is the development of a relatively sterile, low-nutrient lake or stream into one rich in nutrients and filled with aquatic life. Carried on to its ultimate end, it is the process by which a lake will change to a marsh or swamp and, finally, to dry land. It is a natural process which, in the absence of factors working to prevent it, occurs in all bodies of water, but which in most natural situations occurs slowly.

It is not eutrophication in itself that is considered objectionable, but the accelerated form of it which occurs when water pollution goes unchecked. With too rich and continuous an inpouring of nutrients, the growth of aquatic vegetation, such as the various kinds of native algae, becomes excessive. Upon death, they draw down, in the oxidative processes of decay, the level of oxygen in the water, creat-

Even in undisturbed state, the fresh waters support an abundance of native aquatic vegetation. Water lettuce (*Pistia*) in Corkscrew Swamp.

ing anaerobic conditions unfavorable to animal life. In the decay process they may also liberate quantities of other gases—hydrogen sulfide and methane, for example—that make the waters still less suitable for most kinds of life. The presence of exotic water weeds, which happen to grow fast and produce great quantities of plant material, speeds up this process. Thus water bodies become relatively useless for most human purposes, and at times become decidedly obnoxious.

The only long-term solution to most of our problems of pollution involves the recycling of the materials involved. The excess of phosphates and nitrates that is so undesirable in fresh-water bodies or in estuaries is badly needed to enrich the upland soils from which these compounds were, in most cases, originally removed. The process of getting them from the water back up to the soils, however, has thus far been baffling to pollution control experts.

Viewed in one way, exotic weeds, such as water hyacinths, do an excellent job of removing excess nutrients from the waters in which they grow and concentrating them in their plant tissues. If the hyacinths can, in turn, be removed from the waters and transported back to upland areas, these nutrients could be returned to the soil. Pursuing this line of thought, the Florida Governor's Aquatic Research and Development Committee encouraged investigations into the crushing, drying, and pelleting of them for conversion into livestock feed. It was found that when properly processed, hyacinths yielded a palatable, high-protein feed that was quite acceptable to cattle. Furthermore, it was found to be entirely feasible to harvest and process hyacinths in this way as a commercial enterprise. Unfortunately, America's economy is geared to favor waste. What makes good sense ecologically is not necessarily going to be adopted commercially, even if it is potentially profitable.

So long as the existing and conventional sources of livestock feed hold out and meet the existing demands, there will be no rush to develop new sources. Similarly, so long as nitrates can be cheaply produced and phosphates can be mined in quantity, there will be no rush to utilize the organic fertilizers that can be produced in great quantity from sewage treatment plants. Many communities have found that they could not even give away the germfree, odorless, dry, organic fertilizer that they had produced in the belief that they were meeting a national need. Farmers and gardeners are too well accustomed to spreading the regular commercial, inorganic product. As a nation we are too used to washing the wealth from our soils down the river and into the sea.

In consequence, the most commonly used method of hyacinth control is chemical and involves spraying the hyacinths with the hormonal spray 2, 4-D. This kills the plant and clears the surface water. But the dead hyacinths sink to the bottom, adding to the organic debris that chokes the water body, and in decay exhaust the oxygen and release back into the water the nutrients that will support the next big crop of water weeds. However, the process keeps chemical industries happy and provides work for men to do.

When Rodman Pool was created as part of the Cross-Florida Barge Canal destructive process, it quickly became enormously rich in nutrients. These came from the disturbance and oxidation of organic bottomland soils, from the great masses of hardwood forest (5,500 acres) that were crushed into the mud, and from the arresting by the dam of the debris and nutrients that were carried down the Oklawaha River. In 1969, 3,000 acres of the pool were choked by an estimated 300,000 tons of water hyacinths. The cost of battling such quantities of water weeds was one of the many factors not considered in the cost–benefit analysis of the proposed canal carried out by the Army Corps of Engineers. However, from all past evidence it was obvious that water weed control would have been a major activity throughout the length of the barge canal, if it had been built.

Unfortunately, water hyacinths are only the most conspicuous and not the most troublesome of the introduced water weeds. Two species which have appeared more recently in the state show promise of causing much more trouble—the Florida elodea and the Eurasian water milfoil (*Myriophyllum spicatus*). The latter grows equally well in fresh and in brackish water, which creates a double problem. According to the governor's committee, over 3,000 acres of it were established in 1967 in the Gulf at the mouth of the Homosassa River, below the famous Homosassa Springs tourist center. There is nothing to keep it from spreading to bays and estuaries throughout Florida, since it can grow from vegetative parts that are readily picked up and carried by passing boats.

Florida elodea, which has been rated as the fastest-growing submerged aquatic flowering plant in the world, can reproduce and spread in almost every way known—from tubers, runners, or plant fragments. Mechanical control is inadvisable since extreme care must be taken to avoid spreading the infestation. Chemical control, involving heavy applications of copper sulfate, is both highly expensive and not very effective. Enough poison to kill the plant will kill virtually everything else as well. Furthermore, the use of chemical controls for elodea, as well as for hyacinths, only aggravates the problem of eutrophication.

There was little doubt that these water weeds would have joined the water hyacinth in invading the proposed Cross-Florida Barge Canal, if it had by some misfortune been completed. *Hydrilla* is already established in Inglis Pool at the west end of the canal and in the St. Johns River at the eastern end. There seems little to be done to prevent its spread.

One must conclude that unless some remarkable new breakthrough is made in methods of weed control, the best approach to these introduced exotics is to learn to live with them, perhaps find various aquatic animals that will eat them, or if necessary go into the water weed business, using them to clear the waters of nutrient and then harvesting them for use as fertilizer or forage. Florida's fresh and estuarine waters are, even without man's undesirable additions, some of the most highly productive areas on earth.

Their productivity is going into exotics that we have not learned to utilize. Perhaps it is past time that we did.

Although there may be no other final answer to water weeds except to capitalize on them, there is one way to reduce the quantity and extent of their infestation; that is to control the sources of water pollution. In this area it is not lack of ability, but lack of public will, that seems to prevail. The attitude toward treatment of sewage in most Florida communities has been primitive, to use the kindest word. Jacksonville has been pointed out as one of the worst offenders, lacking in some of its metropolitan areas even the most primary level of treatment and dumping raw sewage into the St. Johns River. The lower reaches of the St. Johns have been described by George Reid as "a gigantic sludge tank; it does not flow, it oozes." Jacksonville may be extreme, but it has many rivals. Tampa Bay has been described as a potential disaster area as the result of continued pollution, and major oil spills in this area in 1970 have aggravated an already severe problem. In Collier County, Florida, one after another proposed development receives approval for construction when it is clearly known that only ineffective means for pollution control are available. The need to construct waste treatment systems, preceding or accompanying the construction of residential or industrial buildings, as an integral part of urban development is only recently being considered.

The problem of aquatic weeds, however, does not only illustrate the need for pollution control, but is a dramatic aspect of a general Florida problem that involves the introduction and acclimatization of exotic plants and animals of all kinds. Except for Hawaii, Florida has more trouble with exotic invaders than any other state, and there is no sign that the problems will grow fewer.

Allen Andrews, a pioneer settler at the Koreshan Unity Colony at Estero Bay, south of Fort Myers, has written an account of his early experiences in Florida. (Koreshan Unity was in itself, originally, an interesting Florida exotic: It was a religious group that believed the world to be concave, not convex—a hollow sphere with man dwelling on the inside.) In 1912, Andrews reported planting the first seeds near Fort Myers of a tree called the cajuput (*Melaleuca leucadendron*). He stated that the species had been introduced several years earlier near Miami, by Professor John Gifford, a forester at Miami University. He was most enthusiastic about its prospects as an ornamental and as a tree of many potential uses. It was thought to have, like the Australian eucalyptus, mosquito-repellent qualities and to be of value in drying up marsh- and swampland. Andrews was right about its adaptability. It has long since taken off and moved right across Florida, growing in a variety of sites and displacing many native species of trees.

The *Melaleuca,* like the eucalyptus, is Australian; on its native continent it exists in nearly one hundred different species. It also shares membership with the eucalyptus in the myrtle family. In its homeland it is known as the paperbark tea tree, in part because of its dense, white, peeling, paperlike bark. There it keeps to its place in swampy ground and along the banks of streams. In Florida, in the words of Mary Barrett, it spreads because of "its ability to stand wet ground, dry ground, salt air, small fires, and some frost." Given half a chance, it will invade new ground, taking it over completely, excluding all rivals. This is not a bad characteristic in those areas where the tree is wanted, but it becomes most undesirable when the tree invades parks or other land where the object is to maintain thriving stands of native vegetation. So the *Melaleuca* is not loved, except by gardeners, and it is necessary to maintain vigilance to keep it out of Everglades National Park.

Any bad feelings toward the *Melaleuca,* however, are mild compared to those reserved for its Australian compatriot, the casuarina, the so-called Australian pine. In Australia, casuarinas go under the name of she-oak or bull-pine. They are, however, neither oaks nor pines. Although they have foliage which resembles that of needle-bearing conifers, the impression is misleading since what appear to be leaves of the casuarina are actually green twigs. The trees actually belong with the hardwooded, broad-leaved angiosperms and are members of the beefwood family.

There are three species of casuarina in Florida, two of which are relatively under control and one of which has run wild. Along the canal roads outside of Everglades National Park, and particularly beside the Tamiami Trail leading out from Miami, grows *Casuarina lepidophloia.* Its foliage is dense and dark green, and its appearance from a distance is pinelike. It forms an effective windbreak and tolerates wet soil along fresh-water streams and canals, but it does not tolerate salt spray or brackish water. In northern Florida, its place is taken by the more hardy *Casuarina cunninghamiana,* which occupies similar sites, but is adapted to colder weather. The villain of the piece in southern Florida is *Casuarina equisetifolia,* a seashore tree not just of Australia, but one that is found throughout the tropical western Pacific. In its home countries, it normally forms the first tree layer behind the beach shrubs that fringe open sandy beaches. It also takes a part in succession inland on bare ground created by fire or other disturbance. In such inland sites, however, it is displaced by the broad-leaved evergreen of the climax tropical forests, eventually being shaded out. Its sanctuary is therefore the coastal fringe, where saline soil and salt spray prevent other trees from becoming established. Both quick-growing and prolific, it can quickly form dense stands under which other plants have difficulty becoming established. Coastal Florida seems to favor the development of such uniform stands of casuarina. On Key Biscayne, for example, it has taken over the beach edge and also inland areas that were once occupied by commercial coconut plantations. Hurricane Donna spread the casuarinas down the Gulf beaches and to islands of Everglades National Park, where it has not been welcomed as a competitor with native plants. A dense stand that has grown up on Cape Sable is said to occupy what was formerly the nesting ground of sea turtles on the upper beaches. The National Park Service has belatedly attempted an eradication program.

Sanibel, Captiva, and Jupiter islands all support dense stands of casuarina, and indeed it is now one of the most conspicuous plants of the south Florida coast. All around the Rookery Bay area, the casuarinas are spreading—occupying old Indian mounds, old dunes, spoil banks in the mangrove zone, and nearly every beach edge.

Another tree that is a more recent invader in southern Florida, but shows promise of becoming as troublesome as any, is the Brazilian holly, or Brazilian pepper tree (*Schinus terebinthifolius*). This tree was brought to Florida as a cultivated ornamental because of its shiny leaves and holly-like berries, but it proved well adapted to life in the wild. Birds loved its berries, spreading its seeds everywhere, and it is now joining its fellow exotics in threatening to invade Everglades National Park and other protected areas of natural vegetation.

These are only a few of the long list of exotic plants that are established in Florida. Most of the exotic plants were brought into Florida deliberately because of their value to agriculture or landscape gardening. Most of them have been well behaved in the sense that they stay where they are planted and don't spread rapidly in the wild. Many, however, have moved out as exotic weeds, becoming troublesome, particularly to those who seek to maintain the natural scene, but also as pests in farm lands, managed forests, or pastures.

I have long accepted the idea advanced by Charles Elton that exotic plants tend to invade disturbed areas and are generally unable to establish themselves in mature or climax plant communities. Climax vegetation has an inherent stability, being made up of those species which have adapted themselves in competition with other species to a particular ecological niche, a place in the environment to which they are better adapted than their rivals. An invader has a disadvantage in competing with species which have proved their ability to hold a particular niche over centuries or thousands of years of such competition. Exceptions are to be noted in island communities, particularly those on remote oceanic islands.

The numbers of species that can reach such islands are necessarily limited by their distance from the major evolutionary sources of plants or animals. The degree of competition is thus restricted, and many species occupy areas to which they are not particularly well adapted. Exotics brought by man to such isolated areas can often displace the natives through their superior adaptation to particular sites. However, barring this kind of exception, my own observations indicate that Elton's rule holds up quite well. South Florida, superficially, is an exception.

The climatic climax is the tropical hardwood forest of south Florida's hammocks.

Actually, I believe there is no exception. The climatic climax of Florida, meaning the biotic community best adapted to the regional climate, is the tropical hardwood forest, represented in Florida by hammock forests. This is both complex in number of species and highly stable. I have seen no evidence that such hammocks, where undisturbed, can be invaded by exotics. That they are invaded is evidence of the degree to which disturbance does occur. Fire, hurricane, land clearing, and other activities remove the native vegetation, thus eliminating the competition for exotics, at least temporarily. They hold the ground for a time, but if the disturbance ceases, they will be replaced by the natives. With severe disturbance, however, the characteristics of the site may be changed—soil may be lost, water balances upset, local microclimates permanently modified. Under these circumstances the invaders could hold the ground for a much longer period of time.

The success of exotics results primarily from the unstable nature of much of the terrain in southern and coastal Florida, and this is related in turn to the prevalence of disturbing factors. Thus, the saw-grass marshes of the Everglades remain in saw grass because of the seasonal overflow of lakes and streams in the wet season and their retreat within their banks in the dry. Added to this are the periodic fires which do not harm the saw grass, but eliminate any trees or shrubs that manage to invade the area. Slight changes in elevation in the marsh areas, caused by accumulation of litter or soil, create new habitats not well suited to saw grass, which can then be invaded by native shrubs or by the exotic casuarinas or *Melaleucas*. The suppression of fire, even in the absence of other changes, also permits those woody plants that can stand periodic submergence to move in. Human disturbance—canalization and the creation of spoil banks, for example—creates still more new habitat.

Mangrove swamps, a relatively stable feature of the coast, can be in any one area unstable. They are adapted to the tidal ebb and flow with its effect on the salinity of water and its mechanical disturbance of tidewater plants. Still, because the mangroves often tend to accumulate soil and litter around their roots, they create higher ground above the tides and therefore less suited to their own occupancy and accessible to other invaders. Beach areas are particularly unstable since wind, tide, and storm waves constantly change the shape of the shore. Beach vegetation is shifting in occupancy, and bare sand is always available to invaders. The casuarina is highly adapted to such invasion.

Hurricanes, of course, can completely upset prevailing ecological balances, opening up large areas to occupancy by species that previously could not have displaced the established vegetation. Man's activities, however, are more continuous and widespread in bringing such changes about. Thus much of Florida is wide open to exotics. It remains to be seen, however, how well the exotics can hold the ground once the sites that they occupy become relatively stable. Indeed, the ecology of both exotics and native vegetation and the interrelationships between the two are far more talked about than studied.

To add further to the vulnerability of Florida to the inroads of exotic things is its geographic situation as a tropical borderland. Tropical Florida has much of the isolation of a tropical island, and does not support the full array of species that would grow there if it had land connections with the mainland tropical centers of plant and animal evolution. Many species exist that may be better adapted to its soil and climate than are the species that already occur there —all of which at one time were also exotic invaders in a strange land. This explains more particularly Florida's vulnerability to animal invaders; there is no doubt that many vacant niches have existed in the past, and probably many still exist. Man's introductions of exotic species only hastens to some degree a process that would otherwise occur over a longer period of time. But acceleration of natural processes, whether these be soil erosion, eutrophication, or exotic invasions, can precipitate what we choose to call environmental catastrophes; that is, they can make the environment less useful to human purposes.

In 1968, I received a most unusual telephone call from

the island of Tristan da Cunha in the South Atlantic. Traveling by radio to a ham operator in Maryland and then by telephone to me, it alerted me to a potential threat to Florida. This time it was the possible introduction into the Miami area of the Australian red-backed spider—a venomous little beast said to be worse than, but similar to, the American black widow. The story that follows illustrates the continual potential for trouble involving exotic animals and the need for continued vigilance.

In 1968, the Conservation Foundation was supporting an expedition to Tristan da Cunha, involving the Australian botanist Nigel Wace and the English zoologist Martin Holdgate, for the purpose of learning more about the unique biology of this island group and possibly of establishing an international research center there. The telephone call to me was prompted by the arrival in Tristan of an American satellite-tracking station, which had been moved there from the interior of New South Wales in Australia. The station equipment had been packed up in Australia and trucked to Sydney, where it was loaded on a plane that took it as far as Honolulu. There it remained for a number of days before being loaded onto another plane for Miami. At Miami it remained for a considerable period of time before being taken on a naval-research vessel to Tristan. At Tristan, Wace discovered a thriving colony of red-backed spiders living in the station equipment. Although he believed he had killed them all, thus preventing their establishment on Tristan, he thought it likely that some had escaped in Hawaii, in Miami, and possibly in the hold of the ship. He wished me to alert the necessary authorities so that a "search and destroy" operation could be carried out in those places.

Exotic Things

On calling the various public authorities, I made an interesting discovery. Spiders didn't fit into our governmental
structure. The Department of the Interior was concerned
with birds and mammals, reptiles, fish, and various other
game or commercially valuable species. Agriculture had an
interest in plant quarantine and potential crop-destroying
pests. Public Health was interested in human quarantine
and the destruction of disease vectors. Spiders were none of
these. After some days, however, a spider man was located
and, I trust, took the necessary steps. If you are bitten by a
red-backed spider in Florida though, you will now know
how it got there and why it remained.

In the United States, Florida is second only to Hawaii in
vulnerability to invasion by exotic animals; it is tropical
Florida, for reasons we have already looked at, that is the
most vulnerable. Some of the exotic invasions have been
accidental and follow a common pattern that can be observed around the world. Man's agricultural croplands,
themselves exotic, are a natural habitat for exotic pests.
Thus the Caribbean fruit fly presumably entered Florida
with a shipment of tropical fruit and became established in
the farming counties. The Mediterranean fruit fly has also
sneaked into the state on several occasions and has spread
into the orchards to do damage. Many millions of dollars
have been spent in eradicating these two pests, although it
remains more than likely that they will be introduced again
in the future. Nevertheless, where values are high on inten-
sively managed lands, exotic invaders can usually be controlled. In the wild where the cost of control runs higher
and dollars-and-cents values are less obvious, control becomes much more difficult.

The story of the cattle egret illustrates how natural introductions take place. This is the common, small white egret that may be seen now along roadsides throughout Florida. It resembles the native snowy egret, but the snowy has a black bill and legs, with yellow feet (hence its common name of "golden slippers"), whereas the cattle egret has a yellow bill and legs. The native range of the cattle egret is in southern Europe and Africa. It is the white bird that perches on the back of the buffalo or rhino in African game pictures. It follows game herds or domestic cattle about, feeding on insects that are stirred up by their passage or are attracted by their droppings. For centuries it lived in the Old World and did not appear elsewhere. Then in the 1940s, it arrived in British Guiana in South America. Nobody knew how it had traveled there. In 1952, these birds were reported all along the east coast of the United States. A small flock was seen on Lake Okeechobee by several people, and its identity was positively confirmed. It proceeded to nest there in 1953, and from then on the egrets were off and away. In 1956, over one thousand nests were counted in one area of Lake Okeechobee, but by then the bird was established from New Jersey's coast on the north to Texas on the west and had become one of Florida's most common herons.

It seems likely that the egrets were carried from Africa to Guiana and thence to Florida by storm winds. Nigel Wace on Tristan reported that following a heavy storm in 1968, a number of South American marsh birds appeared on the island. On Tristan, and indeed under most circumstances where storm waifs are carried to other lands, a suitable habitat did not exist, so that the birds could not become established. In Florida, however, there was a wide-open ecological niche for a heron that could adapt to being in a close relationship with man, his domestic animals, and his highway-littering proclivities. However, the cattle egret's success is spectacular, equaled only by that of those early immigrants to the United States, the English sparrow and the common starling.

People like to buy and keep for pets all manner of exotic animals, including a truly remarkable range of exotic fish. From time to time they feel inclined to liberate these creatures, dumping them into a creek or turning them loose in the countryside. Most, fortunately, do not survive; but too many do. Rumors crop up from time to time of giant anacondas living in the hammocks and swamps of the Everglades wilderness. Considering the inclination people have for keeping and turning loose pet snakes, one cannot dismiss these stories entirely as being myths. Others, because of some macabre psychological twist, have liberated the vicious piranha fish from the Amazon basin in Florida waters. Fortunately, they have not survived; but some could. There are reportedly half-wild monkeys living near some Florida homes. Such tropical American wildcats as the jaguarundi and the ocelot have been turned loose in Florida. We have already noted the spectacular success of the armadillo. The South American caiman, which could displace the native alligator, has been liberated. The giant toad from South America, *Bufo marinus,* is now also successfully established. Its large poison glands on its neck have caused the death of scores of domestic dogs that have attacked these toads and bitten into them.

Some of the exotic animals turned loose cause people to choose sides. Thus, the red-whiskered bulbul, a favored pet as a singing caged bird, was accidentally released in the Miami area in the 1950s. It is now well established. Since it is a fruit eater, it is feared as an orchard pest. But since it is an attractive songster, it has its organized friends who oppose government attempts at its destruction. The scarlet ibis, one of the most beautifully colored of all marsh birds, was deliberately introduced by the keeper of a heronry near Miami. Some welcomed it as a worthwhile addition to the bird life of Florida. Others feared that it would interbreed with and imperil the survival of the native white ibis. It does not appear to be surviving in the wild at the present time, but it is difficult to be certain. Our means for monitoring wild areas and animal populations are quite haphazard —in fact were it not for the annual Audubon bird counts, there would be no regular program at all.

The Florida Game and Fresh-water Fish Commission has embarked on a program for liberating game birds— particularly exotic species of ducks—in the hope of enhancing game-bird hunting for Florida sportsmen. Many groups, which favor enhancing the native waterfowl populations instead, are in opposition.

Most recently, the walking catfish, an Asiatic species, has attracted much publicity. Turned loose in Florida waters, it has become well established over what has been estimated as a thousand-square-mile area. This creature can actually get up on its fins and crawl along over dry ground from one body of water to another. The drying up of a pond or marsh does not necessarily affect its survival if there are other fresh-water bodies that it can move to. Fisheries experts are naturally concerned that it may displace more-valuable native fish species, but in fact, there is little to be done. Earl Frye, director of the Florida Game and Fresh-water Fish Commission, has indicated that it may now be impossible to control its spread without doing greater damage through the control efforts than the fish itself would be expected to do.

There are those who would prefer to stop all introductions of exotic creatures into the wilds of America. It is far too late for this. Others, mostly those who know little about the problem, favor a completely open-door policy toward exotics, with survival of the fittest. Only a middle ground makes any sense. Many exotics are valuable, and some are perhaps essential. For example, the insects and other creatures brought in for biological control of various pest species (themselves, for the most part, exotics) are necessary exotics. Various game birds and fish, such as the ring-necked pheasant and the brown trout, are valued exotics. Plants useful in agriculture or in gardens and animals used for meat production are either essential or highly worthwhile. There is no reason to prevent such introductions. There is every reason why the random introduction of species that could cause serious problems to health, to agriculture, or to native fauna or flora should be halted. There is adequate reason to insist upon the careful advance study of each species to be brought in, for controlled testing of such species before liberation into a wild state, and for follow-up studies after the species has been liberated. There is need for strict laws and quarantine procedures to prevent accidental introductions of unwanted species, and need for severe penalties against individuals who liberate exotic species that they have variously acquired. Since Florida is most vulnerable, it requires the strictest controls. At present these are lacking. As for most exotics that are already here, the best we can do is study them and learn from them.

Bald Cypress and Egret

11 : Nobody Is in Charge

TRADITIONALLY, FLORIDA HAS welcomed people and cried out for growth. In this it has differed only in degree from the rest of the United States; it has been somewhat louder in its welcome and more strident in its demand. In the 1960s, some of the more serious effects of these attitudes were felt. In the 1970s, the whole question of Florida growth must be answered. The answer will be of importance to all the world.

Florida has over six million residents today, but in addition, it welcomes an estimated twenty million or more visitors annually. The question of how many people Florida could support and how many tourists it could accommodate is essentially meaningless. The question must be qualified. How many people can Florida support at what standard of living, in what kind of an environment, at what cost to the state, the nation, or the world? These are some of the qualifying phrases. The same qualifications, and others, must be considered in relation to tourism. Florida's answers, and their consequences, will be particularly and immediately important to the islands of the West Indies, since these are faced with the same questions and their survival may depend upon the right answers.

Obviously the Florida environment, like that of the West Indies, provides both a reason for the existence of Florida's problems and a means for determining the answers. People flock to Florida because it seems a better place to live or a more interesting place to visit than other places seem. They do not similarly flock to Mali, Saudi Arabia, or Baffin Island. They seem to be draining out of many areas of the Middle West and the intermountain region. Is it just the climate that attracts people to Florida? How important is fishing in influencing their decision to come? How much do beaches and the warm waters of the seas enter into the equation? Is freedom from the congestion of the great metropolitan areas of the North part of the charm? How important is the natural vegetation and wildlife? How many of those who like trees and birds would be satisfied with plastic palms and aviaries? There have been many surveys that have provided various answers. All suggest that fishing, beaches, natural scenery, and other environmental factors are major determinants in the decision to move to, or visit, Florida. But if this be so, how do we explain the continued, determined assault on the Florida environment and the apparent indifference to the destructive changes that are taking place?

Sometimes I think that all who believe in the values and

charms of the natural environment should be forced to spend a week in Las Vegas. Nobody pretends that the natural environment attracts people to Las Vegas. If it did, we would find the same numbers gathered around the edges of the Black Rock Desert or flocking into Gerlach. In fact, those who arrive in Las Vegas soon disappear into the interior of a luxury hotel from which they emerge only to visit other hotels, clubs, or casinos. They do become exposed to desert sunlight and air around the edge of the hotel pool, which usually does contain natural, if adulterated, water; but their surroundings during this experience are otherwise plastic. The hotels live a life of their own, paying no attention to the biological clocks of their guests. Day and night are little different, except with reference to the timing of the floor shows—there are fewer during daylight. But at all hours, the slot machines whir, and the fall of dice, cards, and counters may be heard.

Those who survive Las Vegas should go to Miami Beach. Here are the same arrays of luxury hotels, spectacular floor shows, outdoor swimming pools, indoor and outdoor bars. There is no legal gambling, which makes a difference. There is an ocean with an ocean beach, but it is mostly for scenery. For the use that is made of it, it could well be replaced with a great, colored photograph. Few people care to get sandy or salty. Anyone who has traveled knows he can go from Los Angeles to Miami, to the French Riviera, the Caribbean, Japan, London, Sydney, and always remain in the same constant environment provided by Conrad Hilton or his rivals. One also knows that millions of people seek out these habitats. I don't know why. Admittedly, there is nothing wrong with having a comfortable, convenient hotel base from which to launch one's expeditions into strange places; but too many persons don't seem to leave the hotels or some artificial environmental equivalent.

One could test the attracting power of the artificial world by removing some of the barriers by which Vegas and Miami Beach are constrained. Create a series of "Sin Cities" that would pander to the widest range of human appetites, place these in the most wretched environmental areas, and then check on the annual attendance and expenditures. This could well be the way in which the Federal Bureau of Outdoor Recreation could arrange to meet the greatest national demand, at minimum cost (or maximum profit), and with the least environmental destruction. (The word *outdoor* would have to be removed from the title.) It could also remove the pressure from our wild areas and satisfy the urge of the bureau to build tourist facilities and access roads.

To be more serious, there is a question as to how much the natural environment means to most people. I don't believe that attendance in national parks, visitor days in national forests, or similar indices are fair measures until we compensate for those people who go to these places for reasons that have little to do with their natural attractions. How do we measure the number of people that visit national parks because of their unique values? Perhaps in the Everglades we could compare the numbers who go straight down the highway without stopping with those who stop, look, and walk around to visit the natural features, the vegetation, and the wildlife that are to be found along the way.

A serious investigation of the concept of "quality of the environment," as it appears to people of various social

The best possible view of Miami Beach. Away from the public park, hotel decks extend to the water's edge.

Even the National Park Service makes ugly mistakes: the trailer camp at Flamingo.

levels, ethnic groups, cultures, and nations, has been proposed by UNESCO as part of its new environmental program. Such a study of human preferences and attitudes needs, of course, to be balanced against a study of environmental realities, against the ecological determinants that set limits to the uses of ecosystems, before it will become meaningful. But such studies must be made; we must have significant and not superficial investigations of this kind before we can reach serious judgments about population levels.

As a part of such investigations, we need look into the proposals that various urbanists have made about cities of the future. Some have suggested enormous vertical cities, towering above the present levels of Manhattan, which could concentrate in an imaginative way all the daily urban wants and needs of people, but would occupy little horizontal space. If these were possible and attractive to people, we could accommodate far greater numbers in much less space than we are accustomed to using. Presumably open space and even wild nature could still be available to those who cared to venture outside. Others have suggested closing our cities off under great domes, within which environmental conditions would be controlled as in a spacecraft. Outside, the natural environment could continue, except for those areas used for automated farms. Still other variations of such futuristic themes suggest linear cities, floating cities, and cities under the sea, all with their concentrations of people and their essential activities. Do such proposals make any ecological sense? Would people tolerate them, or perhaps prefer them to existing arrangements? It could appear that such proposals have some bearing on planning for the future of environment and population in Florida. But to be realistic, it is only with reference to the long-range future, beyond the next critical half-century, that any such proposals have meaning.

The momentum of change must overcome the inertia of history, habit, and environment. Admittedly the momentum has been enormous during the past decade. The rate of change is unprecedented in man's history. But one must also be impressed by the continuance of habit—tracing from history and tradition, as well as from human biology and psychology—and by the resistance of the environment. In the fewer than thirty years that separate us from the year 2000, we are not going to destroy all that we have built and start anew from the ground. The cities of the twenty-first century are already taking shape around us.

In Florida, the Marco Island Development Company, for example, is building a twenty-first-century city on Marco Island and on the mainland and islands to the south, east, and north. It will be a city just like most other Florida waterfront developments with boat canals, detached houses on private lots, some high-rise buildings, some limited access to beaches, and centralized shopping and service areas. It will still be under construction in 1980, hardly fully occupied by A.D. 2000, and still lived in during the twenty-first century unless hurricane, world-wide conflict, or some other catastrophe prevents this. Miami Beach is a much older place, but I see no forces at work to tear down the multimillion-dollar hotels or otherwise change the basic structure of this city. We have some leeway for change, but change will take place in the middle of those basic patterns for land-use that have already been created.

The world of 1970 is not much different from the world of 1930. It is more concentrated, more precarious, more powerful, more vainglorious, and infinitely more nasty, but all its patterns are recognizably similar. By A.D. 2001, we are likely to be the same blend of good and bad, idealistic and perverse, altruistic and self-seeking people that we are today, and all these qualities, along with many more, will be found in each individual.

It is disheartening, from one point of view, to contemplate the idea that we will face the third millennium A.D. with the same contrary natures with which mankind faced the first millennium A.D. As a teen-ager, I read space fiction, but was repelled because the space pilots that it portrayed were not in the least improved psychologically or spiritually from the pirates of the sixteenth century. This I could not accept at the time. Now I must. Our astronauts of today are stalwart, intrepid individuals, but so were the officers who led the Roman legions in their invasion of Britain, and so were those who charged at Balaklava. Our astronauts are better informed. It is unfortunate that information has so little influence upon behavior. We must, I fear, face tomorrow with the human material and the natural environment that we have today.

To return to the relationship of these ideas to the question of Florida's population and environment, it is obviously not possible to speak of overpopulation in Florida in a general sense. Yet, in a relative sense, Florida today appears seriously overpopulated. In operation, the question of population can be evaluated only in relationship to two other factors: the control over technology and the control over land-use. It is the complex of population–technology–land-use that creates today's problem in Florida, and in the United States, and causes us to speak of overpopulation and the need for population control. With a different arrangement of people and different controls over their activities, we could perhaps not have to speak of over-population. But we are faced with today's peoples, today's technology, and today's land-use.

The need for control of population growth in Florida is real, not because there are necessarily too many people nor because population has necessarily exceeded some optimum level, but because numbers of people and their rate of growth through births and immigration make it difficult or nearly impossible to solve the problems involving the control of technology and land-use. Technological expansion with its so-called side effects, of which the most serious is pollution, contributes to enormous deterioration of the environment. Misplaced land-uses disrupt the entire environment. Population growth, and the need to accommodate it, is used as an excuse for setting aside the rules, or not writing the rules, that would protect the environment: "We must have more jobs. We must attract industry. We must provide housing . . . or schools, or roads, or power plants because population growth must be accommodated." Thus populations grow without control and are encouraged to grow further while the conditions for life become increasingly chaotic and less and less tolerable. Florida is overpopulated, and we could solve the problem by restricting growth, but we could also solve it by controlling our technology and by controlling land-use.

In 1960, Collier County had a population of slightly less than sixteen thousand. This represented an enormous increase from 1950—142 percent. I do not know what the 1970 census will show, but the increase has been great. Still, I would be surprised if the population exceeded one hundred thousand. All these people could easily be ac-

commodated in a small, pleasant, tree-lined, garden city on
the coast. With proper control over pollution, with emphasis on nonpolluting forms of transportation, with the
development of environmentally planned transportation
corridors, the environmental impact of such a city could be
neutral or positive. With adequate arrangement of recreational space, and with facilities ranging from intensive development of mass-recreation amenities to proper control
over wilderness use, all these people could find the outdoor
activities that they preferred with a minimum of adverse
environmental effects. There would be space for the annual
influx of tourists. Most of Collier County's two thousand
square miles could be wild country. Large areas could be in
carefully protected reserves, maintained for their value to
the functioning of the natural systems of water, land, air,
and life—the local contribution to the maintenance of the
world biosphere. Other areas could be variously developed
for agriculture or other forms of commercially productive
land-use. In other words, Collier County is not near any
saturation point of population—if Collier County were
properly managed. But it is not. Considering the existing
degree of control over technology and land-use, considering the absence of any environmentally oriented planning,
Collier County is severely overpopulated, and any increase
in human numbers under these conditions need be viewed
with horror. Collier County is being destroyed or battered
by the existing population–technology–land-use complex.

Why have conditions reached this sorry state? One answer is easy and simple. Nobody is in charge. Neither Collier nor any other Florida county nor the state of Florida
has the leadership that is needed. This does not reflect upon
any elected or appointed official, upon any legislator or

administrator. It does reflect upon the way things are organized. In operation, there are many people in charge. Somebody is in charge of public roads, another in charge of zoning, another responsible for wildlife or fish, national parks, water supply, public health, or pollution control. Nobody is in charge of the environment. Nobody is responsible for control of the population–technology–land-use complex.

Although many factors are involved in the development of the present situation—local governments until recently exercised and needed to exercise little authority—there is one element that affects government at all levels. The fragmentation of responsibility is both a result of and a cause of our emphasis on specialization. In the past, specialization has provided the means by which industrial civilization has moved forward; in the present, it can contribute to its downfall unless its weaknesses are realized.

The Bureau of Public Roads in the Department of Transportation, or its various state counterparts, obviously needs and will continue to need specialists in civil engineering and various types of structural engineering. It also draws on a limited range of other specialists to assist in the task of survey, design, and construction of roads, highways, and their accessory structures. The highway builders, in my observation, have viewed their tasks in simplistic terms: they move people at minimum cost, maximum permissible speeds, and reasonable personal safety from one point where they are concentrated to another where they desire to go; or more importantly, they move goods and materials from their place of production to their place of distribution. In these goals the highway builders are fully supported by those businesses and industries that share the same aims, and to a considerable degree, by the motoring public.

These primary considerations have taken precedence over all others. The cheapest, fastest, safest route is favored, and the agency men will defend it bitterly and doggedly, as though their professional reputations, careers, livelihoods, and indeed the future of mankind were dependent upon public acceptance of this route. And therefore they do some abominable things. For example, I-75, part of the interstate highway system in Florida, was planned to run from Tampa to Miami on a route that cut diagonally across the Big Cypress Swamp and the Everglades, thus cutting a new transportation swath through this wild country and opening it still further to development. It would create a barrier to water movement, introduce a new source for pollution into southward flowing waters, and completely shatter the wilderness characteristics of an extensive area. Not one of these factors appeared to be considered in the plans for its construction. The engineers and economists of the department had not been asked to consider the most environmentally desirable route. Indeed they had not been asked to consider the environment at all, except insofar as it influenced their costs and specifications for building and maintenance.

It is easy to pick on engineers because they create such big, conspicuous, and long-lasting environmental catastrophes. Other specialists are equally to blame, and I would include many of the environmental specialists who gear themselves to game or fish production, to park planning, to forest production, to the establishment of recreational facilities, or to other single, or narrow-purpose, goals. They consistently behave as though all values other than their own were inconsiderable and do not seem to realize that it may be better to have fewer deer and more bluebirds, fewer salmon in the cannery but more dolphins in the seas, fewer boat ramps and more undisturbed woodlands.

Thus the Florida State Department of Natural Resources and the National Park Service could both be tarred with the same brush as the real-estate developers, since they have also constructed canals, for recreational purposes, that upset water balances and created important environmental damage. The national park road from Everglades headquarters to Flamingo creates a paved transportation slot through the park that should never have been permitted. By its very existence it encourages other highway planners to think of its possible extension over Florida Bay as an alternate route to Key West. It adds nothing to the park except as the park is viewed as a boat-launching site for people in a hurry. The national park trailer camp at Flamingo is as atrociously ugly as any trailer camp in Florida, and the area in which the park service personnel are forced to live is a disgrace. But the National Park Service should hardly be singled out for blame, since it is not the worst offender. One could make a long list. Admittedly the environmental specialists seldom can create as massive a blunder as the Cross-Florida Barge Canal, but to the extent that they also fail to consider the entire spectrum of the environment, they make their share of mistakes.

It is impossible for our society to live without specialists. We must have the very best that we can train. But where we make our mistake is in asking them to recommend or deliver judgments in areas in which they are not qualified to act.

As I have noted earlier, there is nothing inherently wrong with the Army Corps of Engineers. But the Corps should not be asked to recommend whether a canal should be built, a waterway dredged, or a river dammed. They should not be permitted to carry out final cost–benefit analyses on projects from which their agency will benefit or be put in a position of advocacy on any public work in which they would be involved. To ask any agency, public or private, to be judge or monitor of its own activities is to invite disaster.

It will be argued immediately that neither the Corps nor the Department of Transportation nor any state or county agency makes the final decision. This is left to Congress or the legislature or the county commission after some intermediate review by the Bureau of the Budget or its local equivalent. It can also be pointed out that the heads of various specialized agencies are usually not themselves specialists, but commonly political appointees or administrators who presumably should represent the public interest. But this is sophistry. In fact, the balance is tipped by the supposedly expert advice of the agency specialists. No other agency, and certainly not the legislature, has the time, competence, or access to the data to permit them to develop an equally impressive argument on the contrary side.

Agricultural technology is an example of a modern technology which has moved forward, until very recently, virtually without control from anyone representing a different point of view. The availability of cheap and supposedly effective chemical pesticides since World War II led to countless individual decisions on the part of farmers who were beset by the loss of profits occasioned by the ravages of agricultural pests. To seek expert advice, farmers turned to the farm advisers of the land-grant colleges, or their state or federal equivalents. But since these too were usually specialists with the same bias in favor of more crops per acre and with no training or mandate to consider other values, their advice was predictable. In consequence, farmers have used poisons on their lands which have subsequently been transported to accomplish major environmental damage. The consequences may well be the most significant environmental catastrophe in history. The results are only partially on record, and the long-term effects cannot yet be predicted with any certainty.

There is no convincing evidence that the use of broad-spectrum, persistent pesticides would provide long-term enhancement of agricultural productivity. Their effects have usually not been weighed in the absence of the accompanying use of sophisticated fertilization programs and improved overall technology. There is growing evidence that they fail to control the target pests, and indeed in many places have set in motion plagues of insects that would not have occurred had pesticides of these types not been used. Nevertheless, since they are cheap and easy to use, they continue to be used, and the damage goes on. Obviously, now, the decision to develop and disperse such poisons should not have been left up to the chemical industries which profit from them, nor to the agricultural specialists and farmers who believed that they might profit. But our existing systems have not allowed other means for decision-making.

It is in the field of land-use that the most complete chaos prevails. The state of Florida at the present time does not really know what situation exists in relation to its wild lands and wild species. It does not really know what areas are unique and priceless and which are relatively commonplace. It does not know what areas must be kept essentially in a natural condition in order to guarantee the long-term survival and functioning of the land and water ecosystems on which human well-being will depend. It knows little and has taken few positive steps to acquire this knowledge, even though most of it is available here and there in the hands of various individuals, institutions, or in published literature. Within Florida, no county government has yet acquired the environmental knowledge on which to base decisions, and few if any are making efforts to obtain it. In consequence, major land-use decisions affecting the total environment are made, essentially at random, by private individuals or groups or agencies that are seeking only to advance their own supposed material well-being or the prestige of their organization. Government exercises little effective control over this process, and communities, counties, and the entire state represent a hodgepodge of conflicting, private, and in their totality, chaotic and unintelligent land-use decisions.

Individuals or groups who seek to make money from land development usually operate initially in complete secrecy, moving to buy tracts of land without setting in motion rumors or speculation that would cause the price of that land to rise. When the land has been secured, development plans may also be produced in relative secrecy. Not until plans are airtight and secure from competition does the public become aware of what is going to take place. A brief notice in the newspaper will call attention to a rezoning hearing at the planning commission meeting that will effect lands specified as being in a particular township, range, and section. Since few people have township, range, and section maps available, few will be aware of which lands are being considered. Most commonly no opposition to the change in zoning will appear at the hearing. Unless planning experts have previously studied the area in question, the commission is likely to be overwhelmed by the array of facts presented by the developer and the glowing prospect of potential new tax money coming into the county treasury. The zoning change and later the subdivision plan are likely to receive approval without a demurring vote. Most commonly in Florida, the commission will itself be representative of those development interests that turn out the vote at local elections while the general public looks in bored indifference at the list of candidates and decides to go golfing or boating instead of voting. Even if environmental protection groups become aware of what is likely to happen through a proposed development, they will rarely have time to gather the facts or carry out the investigations needed to develop an effective opposition to it. There is, in consequence, in most of Florida, no effective control by those who favor environmental quality over the actions of those who seek primarily to improve their private wealth.

Indeed the whole course of private development of land in Florida has been a national disgrace, and despite some efforts at control, it remains a disgrace. Organizations such as the Gulf American Corporation, which advertised itself as Florida's major land developer and one of the state's major employers, have seriously damaged enormous areas of Florida land. Much of western Collier County, when viewed from the air, shows a rectangular network of roads and drainage ditches, spoil banks, and canals; these cut through what was once wild country, without any thought for natural drainage patterns, without consideration of surface or subsurface water flow, without care for potential pollution disasters or the effects on the bays and estuaries, indeed, without care for man, beast, or plant, except to the degree that these could enhance land-development profits.

Gulf American started initially by building what was supposed to be a showplace at Cape Coral, near Fort Myers. Here, and in various other scenic spots, the movies and slides were prepared which showed how anyone could buy a share in a tropical paradise in Florida. All over the country, the corporation then started its hard-sell and soft-sell techniques. Initially, the prospective customer might be invited to a free dinner and cocktails at some relatively prestigious restaurant (of course, with no obligation or commitment implied). There he would be shown the movies or slides purporting to illustrate the new development (Golden Gate Estates or the Remuda Ranch Grants) and informed of the golden opportunities that awaited those who wished to buy retirement or investment property in Florida. Those who took this bait would next be invited to take advantage of what amounted to a nearly free vacation in Florida to look over the land they were to buy. Other prospective customers responded to advertisements promising three days in Florida, including air fare, meals, lodging, and entertainment for only $59.95. Indeed they would be shown the land, from high in the air, and then shown more glorious pictures, subdivision maps, glowing forecasts of potential future trends for the area, all leading to enrichment of those who were "in on the ground floor."

In fact, the major areas, purchased from the Collier Corporation, were poorly suited to individual residential development. Those who purchased lots would not find the land any more than marginally attractive, at best, from the viewpoint of water, soil, vegetation, or any other quality. Many persons were sold underwater lots that could not be drained. In some cases the same lot was sold to more than one individual (on time payments a certain percentage of people will default, so that in an emergency, a switch can be made with appropriate apologies and even minor com-

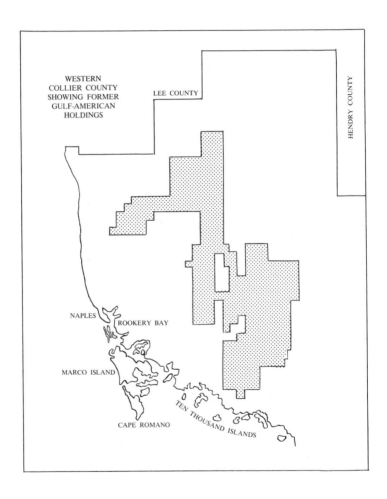

pensation). Under the best of circumstances, those who bought lots found there was no guarantee of any public service in the future: neither power nor light, water nor sewage, effective road systems, nor any other facilities. But after free meals and lodging, a free, or nearly free, plane ride, the general air of good fellowship, followed by the hard sell in the closed office with a public address system reporting the rapid disappearance of purchase opportunities ("We just happen to have one lot left in that tract, and if you hurry, you can just manage to get it") it was indeed difficult for a confused, potential retiree from the Middle West to go away without buying something.

During the process by which Gulf American purchased and subsequently chopped up and began to sell this land, where were the guardians of the public interest? In fact, the Collier County Commission leaned over backwards to give the Gulf American Corporation every assistance. At the height of the scandal that ultimately developed over their operations, it just so happened that the president of Gulf American was also the head of the state of Florida Land Sales Board, an organization that was supposed to oversee and control his own activities. This was a particularly glaring case of the fox being assigned to watch the chickens—a common Florida practice. Conservationists did make an effort to encourage federal purchase of the Fahkahatchee Strand, a unique cypress area, but failed, and Gulf American became its custodian. Fortunately, when Governor Kirk took office, the crackdown on Gulf American began. It was eventually sold to the General Acceptance Corporation, which is at least making the right sounds about having a concern for the environment. But we must wait to see.

Gulf American, however, was not Florida's worst land-sale agency, but only the biggest. All over Florida, similar organizations, small and large, are using the same approaches—selling land to gullible customers in areas that are worthless for development, but priceless as wild country or for uses other than as residential lots. Telephones ring day and night to start the selling process. Customers are lured to the free dinners, plane rides, and to entertainments at the "country clubs" to which they will have automatic membership upon purchase of their lot. Despite laws that require disclosure of the various limitations to the development of a "Florida homesite," it is estimated that 22,500 units of Florida land, unusable for residential purposes, are sold by telephone from Miami in each year. The great medicine show goes on, the barkers are in full cry, and in the process the state of Florida is being destroyed.

The existing legal means for control of land-use have been proved effective in those areas where they are least needed and most ineffective in situations where they are desperately required. Zoning of land for particular purposes holds up quite well until major profits are to be made from rezoning. Then, for reasons fair or foul, zoning tends to break down—agricultural land becomes open to urban development, residential land suddenly becomes commercial, and so on. The idea of the purchase of easements for conservation purposes—the purchase of certain development rights to hold land in a particularly desirable form of land-use—seemed a good way around the land-use control dilemma at one time. One can easily buy at small cost from a landowner his right to do something he had no intention of doing. The government can purchase such rights in areas where the prospect for development is remote. But if a lot that is worth a hundred dollars as agricultural or recreational land is likely to become worth three thousand dollars as residential land tomorrow, then purchase of development rights will cost virtually as much as purchase of the land in fee simple.

Taxation can be used by government to inhibit certain kinds of development and to encourage other land-uses. One can, for example, offer a tax incentive to hold land in agriculture; this sometimes helps for a while. But once the development of land brings serious promise of high profits, the threat of higher taxes seldom inhibits its sale for development purposes.

Taxing policies have been most useful in encouraging the donation of land to public agencies for conservation purposes, through permitting the value of such donations to be deducted from income that would otherwise be taxable. Many public or private conservation reserves have been developed from such donations, but obviously only those who are wealthy or have high incomes can take advantage of these tax provisions.

Taxation could also be used to control land speculation and the escalation of land values. The profit from land sales could be essentially removed, or all profits from land sales could be taxed at the same rate as income from salaries and wages and all loopholes that permit avoidance of such taxation could be firmly sealed. If this could be done, it would no longer be necessary for conservation agencies, public or private, to chase behind skyrocketing land prices in their efforts to protect the public environment. But, with existing court interpretation of the rights of landowners, it seems sheer fantasy to dream of using taxation policy in this way.

Zoning, easements, subdivision regulations, the use of

permits to control development (as in lands subject to the
Bulkhead Act), and taxation policies are all tools at the
disposal of public agencies to control the misuse of land.
All of them need to be skillfully employed, and all of them
could be helpful to the public cause. In communities oriented toward protecting the environment, these tools seem
to work fairly well. In those oriented toward development,
where real-estate speculators sit in positions of public
power, they seem not to work at all.

It has been often stated that the only permanent safe-
guard for areas that must be protected lies in purchase of
the lands. By this means, many of the parks, reserves, and
other conservation areas have been set aside. But this
method works poorly when the appropriation of public
funds lags behind the need for public purchase—a situation
that commonly prevails. It also works poorly when the escalation of land values results in the appropriation of funds
falling short of the necessary purchase price. There are
several ways around this dilemma.

Governments can exercise the right of eminent domain
and simply take over title to the land with a just compensation to the landowner. But the purpose for which the land
is taken must be a clearly demonstrated public need, so that
many agencies have hesitated to consider environmental
protection as being in this category. Furthermore, public
funds for compensation must be available.

Private agencies, such as the Nature Conservancy, can
move in ahead of government and buy up options on land
that will ultimately be purchased by government. This can
result in substantial savings if the private agency can buy
land before prices begin to climb. But this requires a commitment on the part of government if the private agency is

not to run the risk of becoming a major landholder. Usually by the time that commitment is forthcoming, land prices have gone up. Furthermore, the funds available to the Nature Conservancy or other private bodies are always inadequate by comparison with total public needs.

A third means that is available for land-use control is that which involves land purchase by a government body with subsequent leaseback or sale back to private ownership. Under the terms of the lease or the sale contract, use of the land can be strictly controlled to conform with the land-use plan or policies of the public agency. Thus, the federal government could buy the entire Ten Thousand Islands area for conservation purposes. Subsequently, it could lease or sell certain areas for use as recreation villages or for other desirable uses. The income from the lease or sale of land for such development purposes could help compensate for the total land cost to the government since the value of such developed areas would be enhanced by the existence of the surrounding conservation reserve. This technique, however, has not as yet been widely employed.

By whatever device it is accomplished, there is an absolute need for public acquisition of many additional areas in Florida. Several of these have already been mentioned: Lignum Vitae Key, the remaining private lands in Everglades National Park, the Ten Thousand Islands, the private lands in the Key Deer and White Heron refuges, the lands needed to protect the remaining wild river systems, and many areas yet to be clearly identified, including the essential sections of the Big Cypress region and of the northwestern Florida Gulf coast.

However, all the devices and techniques that must now be employed to protect the public interest with benefits accruing to the speculator or exploiter are onerous and should be unnecessary. One is forced to conclude that the concepts of "private" land and the "rights of land ownership" as they are now interpreted form a dangerous myth. Far from being long established in Western tradition, they are of relatively recent origin.

The expression of the rights of land ownership in the feudal estates of Europe was tempered by the concept of the duties of landowners. Under the more responsible members of the aristocracy or landed gentry, a concern for the future was expressed with their desire to pass on to their heirs lands that were in better condition than those originally inherited. The great private estates of nineteenth-century England were private in a sense, but the private rights were tempered by a sense of duty to *family past* and *family future*, as well as to all those who were dependent in one way or another upon the estate. Admittedly this old system was subject to abuse, but those who abused it ran the risk of social ostracism at a time when acceptance was deemed important.

The modern anonymous system of land ownership, exemplified in too much of Florida, places a maximum emphasis on rights and a minimum on duties. Public interference with such private rights has been severely resented and has usually been effectively prevented. Yet, in a real sense, there can be no moral right of an individual to hold exclusive power over land. At best, he has a lifetime trusteeship over a property upon which others must ultimately depend. This implies a moral duty to pass land down unimpaired or even enhanced in its value. The land of America must support or enrich the lives of all Americans now and in the centuries to come. It is limited in extent, and the demands that must be placed on it will not diminish but grow. No person can claim the right to impair the livelihood or well-being of future generations through his misuse of the land. This is the moral situation. The legal situation, as we have seen, is of a different order.

Nobody familiar with the heavy-handedness of government would recommend the socialization of land. The finest traditions of land-care have been passed down in private ownership, and we have already noted several Florida examples. Poor management of land is not strictly a private phenomenon; it is often demonstrated on publicly owned land. Nevertheless, the most completely destructive handling of land has usually been done by private owners or by those who develop private land for the benefit of the owners. Much of the development that has taken place in Florida either should not have taken place at all or should have occurred in a different form. There is need to move toward a legal system that will reward the private owner who cares for his land and that will abrogate the rights of those who misuse or destroy land. For the present, every legal device that is available to accomplish this end should be employed.

To sum up, it is pointless to speak of a population problem as though it were the key to Florida's troubles. Florida is overpopulated, but only because land-use and technology go without effective control. Under the circumstances, one can only recommend a three-pronged approach: slow down population growth in order to buy time to gain control over land-use and technology; institute increasingly rigid controls over land-use and move toward a system under which lands must be used for their highest public purpose; and above all, at every level of government institute an agency with concern for and responsibility over the total human environment. Ultimately there could be room for more people in Florida, if such growth were to be considered desirable. Today, with present controls, further population growth must be regarded as disastrous.

To develop a clearer understanding of optimum population levels for Florida, assuming the ability to develop the needed controls, we must begin to know what people actually look for in the way of high-quality environment. It is pointless to ask them, since they do not know. They must be able to see and comprehend the options available. Few can do this at the present time. They must be presented with the balance sheet of losses and gains attendant upon their environmental decisions. Most of all, they must be shown the limits of the earth, the ecological realities that in the long run dictate the rules that humanity must obey.

Loxahatchee River

12 : Repairs for the System

IN TOO MANY PARTS of Florida, it is still easy to be complacent. You can look around and see that the world, in your corner, is still beautiful. You can persuade yourself that it will last out your lifetime, and then, following the tried-and-true "cop out," can say, "Yes, of course, it will change, but who am I to say what kind of world my children will want? They may not want any part of the natural environment!" You can get by with this if you stay in your corner. But don't take a plane trip, or if you do, don't look down. Don't drop in at your friendly neighborhood developer's and look at his plans. Don't check to see what your department of public roads or the Corps of Engineers have up their sleeves. Don't talk to anyone who knows. Because it won't last out your lifetime unless you are planning to die very soon. And your children will have no choice.

It is not the changes that have already occurred that need worry you. It is the accelerating rate of change that is so difficult and so important to comprehend—the knowledge that more will occur during the next ten years than took place during the last one hundred and that this change will take place in a state where there are no longer the great open spaces which you could once trade off to buy time. This is your dilemma, and whether you are a retiree or a young parent or an aspiring student, its solution will affect you. The decisions are yours, and their consequences you must live with. If you abdicate, don't vote, don't participate, don't become informed, then your friendly neighborhood developer will decide what will happen to you, and you will live in the mold that he forms for you.

Realization of the critical nature of our environmental problems and impatience with efforts to accomplish change through traditional means have led many to subscribe to radical viewpoints that admit no halfway measures. At one extreme are those who, rejecting all government, seek to go back to living communally on the land, firm in their belief that human shortcomings result most commonly from the operation of the system—the combination of big technology and big government. They seek to achieve some new and more harmonious state of interaction with nature. One can't help but sympathize with some of these new communards, and wish them well. If they had enough knowledge or were willing to learn, they could well develop new ways of living with the land and with each other that could hold out hope for the future of the human race. But with the environment under as much pressure as it is at the present time, it is difficult to sit by while large groups of people go out into our wilder lands and repeat every land-use mistake that has been made since man first took up agriculture. Many seem engaged in the same process of land despoilation that characterizes the most backward peasantry in the most underdeveloped country. For example, the goat, the great land destroyer of all time, is a depressingly common animal on too many of the new communes.

Differing from those who would retreat to the land are those who wish to overthrow the existing system and replace it with something new. Unfortunately, the new approach most commonly resembles the old, traditional Marxist–socialist approach. We are asked to believe that a new government, led not by the Nixons or Johnsons, but by fiery-eyed, bearded young men in the Ché Guevara pattern, will lead our way to some new utopia. But nobody who has worked in the international environmental area can develop much confidence in this proposal. The Russians, Chinese, Cubans, Algerians, and even the Swedes are all caught in the same environmental dilemma as the United States. If there is an easy way out, not one of these nations has found it.

It does seem strange to an American to hear a Russian complain about the way the lumber industries have been ruining Lake Baikal. He appears to be up against the same troops that operate in our Pacific Northwest, guided by the same pursuit of the dollar for the company till. But in truth, no profit motive is involved for the Russian. Nevertheless, the director for Soviet timber production and the leader of an American timber enterprise are truly brothers. Each seeks to produce more and better forest products for his organization, and, as a consequence, to reap the credit, prestige, power, and privilege that accompany such achievement. Profit, in the capitalist sense, is quite irrelevant. Production, however, means achievement of goals.

Respect for the broader environment may indeed be more important to the Weyerhaeuser Corporation than to its Soviet or Chinese counterpart. But then, the Chinese, the Cubans, or the Algerians can claim that economic development must come first, at all costs, if their nations are to survive. Concern for the environment, supposedly, comes later. Unfortunately, there can be no "later" if the environment is destroyed.

In the socialist countries, we identify the same phenomena that have been observed in Florida. Specialists or those with specialized interests make recommendations aimed at the achievement of their special goals. Above them, in theory, are the leaders, the administrators who should be able to take the overall view. But these are only specialists grown larger. Nobody has impressed on them the need for an environmental view, nor would they be rewarded for taking such a view. In the socialist environment as in the capitalist environment, there is nobody in charge.

It is necessary to mention one final group of environmental activists of the 1970s, since they are so numerous. These are the "Pogo" people. To them, the individual is the key to our environmental dilemma. To them, there is no point in talking about reform of institutions until the individual is reformed. This, of course, places the achievement of environmental sanity in the same unattainable category as the conversion of all people to the Buddhist ideal. But their battle cry is the immortal sentence of Walt Kelly: "We have met the enemy and he is us." This is pleasing to the ears of those who would gut the American land or produce the pollutants that would finish us all. Let those who care about the environment stay home, clean up their own backyards, quit smoking, put bricks in their toilets to save water, give up their cars (and therefore attend fewer public meetings), and generally seek to be very, very good. After all, the big polluters are no worse than the little people who go around defecating, urinating, and exhaling carbon dioxide into the atmosphere. If this be recognized, they can get on with the business of building bigger and better pollution devices for the nonenlightened and burying more estuaries under silt.

I regret to announce that we have no sensible choice other than trying to make the system that we have work better. At the same time, we must crack down with the greatest vigor on those who perpetuate the practices that have brought about the present deterioration of the environment. Obviously part of the job is to get better men to take over the positions of leadership, and that is up to the voters. Part of the job, however, is more fundamental. We need different political and legal devices and controls. We need to abandon some viewpoints that have long been regarded as sacred by those who happen to hold them, and our attitude toward the rights of land ownership is among the first that should go.

Perhaps first of all, we must take the decision-making authority, or the power to exercise a major influence upon decisions, away from those who would in any way benefit from the decision. That is an easy statement to make but one that is difficult to interpret. For instance, illustrating with the controversial barge-canal case, the Corps of Engineers should not be permitted a major voice in deciding whether a canal should be built or what route it should follow. Its role should be confined to fact-finding within its area of competence prior to the decision to build a canal. If

All waterfront development need not be ugly.

the construction should be authorized, it could then assume its role as the agency supervising the construction; in this role, its competence is not under question. Other agencies with special competence need also be brought into fact-finding investigations at an early stage, not after a route has been selected and a decision has been made to go ahead. The recommendation to build a canal and the final selection of a route along with various environmental specifications must be made by an agency that in no way will benefit from the decision and that is as remote as possible from any political pressure. The decision must be based upon a review of the entire situation and all the consequences and alternatives. The final decision must ultimately be made by the Congress, the legislature, county commission, or city council.

The kind of agency that is needed has indeed been established already at the federal level by the National Environmental Policy Act. This is the Council on Environmental Quality, although admittedly the existing council is neither funded, staffed, nor authorized to do the job that is needed and is burdened with other time-consuming duties. Nevertheless such a body could function in the way that is required. One means of ensuring that it is not overridden by executive authority or by congressional action is to require that all its recommendations be fully publicized. A further necessity would be to insist that a decision by the chief executive or by Congress running contrary to the recommendations of the council be also fully publicized so that the public can understand both the original recommendations and the reasons why they were not accepted. This would allow the political influence of the public to be fully exercised, either immediately or at the polls.

It is essential that the same procedure apply to both public agencies and private organizations where their activities would involve any major environmental change. Thus the decision of Florida Power and Light to build a nuclear power plant or the decision of a group of entrepreneurs to develop a high-rise complex on twenty acres would be equally subject to the recommendations of an environmental review board at the appropriate level of government. Obviously, local decisions should be subject to the recommendations of a city or county board; those affecting broader areas, by a state board or the federal council.

Obviously the creation of such boards would place a great deal of political influence in the hands of a single agency at the local, state, or federal level. It would also remove much influence and authority from agencies that now possess these qualities. However, it would take influence from agencies that have much to gain from a decision and place it with one that has nothing to gain by approval or disapproval of any development or practice.

The staffing of environmental review boards is, of course, an important concern. It is impossible to find ecological paragons to fill these influential spots. It would be possible, however, to include on the board or its staff a wide range of environmental expertise either as salaried personnel or as independent consultants. It would also be possible to exclude those with any visible conflicts of interest.

This is not, of course, a new recommendation. I have made it in various forms before and so have many others. Some states and even counties have taken at least preliminary steps to implement it, but all fall short of providing it with the necessary funds, staff, and authority. It is no cure-all for environmental problems, but it can represent a major step towards finding a cure.

A second fundamental problem that requires attention is the remedying of our high degree of ecological ignorance. We do not yet know enough about the ecosystems of the world, about the functioning of the biosphere, and rhetoric cannot for long substitute for knowledge. Support of environmental research at every level is fundamental to the maintenance of a balance between man and his environment. To date such support has not been forthcoming, and in 1970, despite all the words spoken in favor of environmental concerns, such support had fallen to its lowest level in many years. Some years ago, a major international research program was launched—the International Biological Programme. It could have provided many of the an-

All waterfront homes need not look alike.

It is possible to use wild country without destroying it.

swers that we need today and will need more urgently tomorrow. In fact, it has languished for lack of money and lack of enthusiastic support. Few people have heard of it. Now another chance is available through more favorable intergovernmental auspices in such programs as the Man and the Biosphere Programme being developed by UNESCO, to be carried out in a coordinated way by the member states of the United Nations with support from the various UN agencies. If adequate support is provided, and it will need several hundreds of millions of dollars, we may find some badly needed answers to those dilemmas that confront us today. Are we, in truth, in danger of running out of oxygen on this planet? Is there a strong chance that through continued production of carbon dioxide or particulate pollutants, we will bring about a major, adverse, climatic change? What effects are our present activities having on the long-term future of oceanic life? We do not know the answers, but they may be required for our survival.

At the Florida level, there is a distressing degree of ignorance about the organization, structure, and functioning of the ecosystems of which the state is composed. A beginning toward achievement of the knowledge we need would be an environmental inventory. Equally vital, considering the rate at which changes occur, would be a regular program for environmental monitoring to check up at frequent intervals, if not continuously, on the progress of activities that can have drastic effects on the Florida environment. The importance of this cannot be overstressed, since developments have a way of sneaking past county commissions or even proceeding illegally. There are far too few personnel in the field who are trained to detect infringements of environmental laws and regulations and able to act promptly to enforce the laws. A "spy in the sky" for Florida is needed to assist law enforcement agencies in their work and to inform public agencies of conditions that could become serious if allowed to develop.

Remote sensing techniques can detect pollution, can register declines in the health of vegetation, and can readily record any of the more obvious forms of development activity, as well as a wide range of other phenomena of environmental interest. The state of Florida would do well to cooperate with the National Aviation and Space Agency in their development of an environmental monitoring program that makes use of satellites and ground stations. Closer to home, a regular program for aerial monitoring by county and state governments could do much to alert the appropriate authorities of developing troubles. Since one can see very little from the ground in Florida, it is easy to be lulled into a sense of security when a screen of roadside vegetation conceals the environmental mayhem in the back-blocks.

In addition to the new agencies that have been proposed, much needs to be done to streamline and better coordinate the existing agencies. It is patently absurd to have a planning commission grant approval for a development before the state pollution control agency has approved the provisions for control of sewage effluent or other potential pollutants, but this is a common procedure. Only where the Bulkhead Act becomes involved in waterfront development is there a systematized procedure that includes approval by county, state, and federal authority in any reasonable sequence, and even this is often circumvented either by a decision to ignore environmental problems at these various levels of government or by the intervention of the courts to protect the developers' so-called rights.

There is an absolute need for city, county, and state governments to build up highly competent environmental staffs and particularly to develop planning departments with a high degree of environmental competence. Long-range, environmentally oriented planning is the only means for guiding development in any political jurisdiction. It is deplorable that those planning agencies that do exist generally lack the requisite environmental skills for ecologically oriented planning, and many jurisdictions lack even the conventionally trained planners that they require.

It is, of course, to be recognized that even with environmental review boards, research, inventories, monitoring, and efficiently functioning agencies staffed with the necessary range of experts, problems will continue to arise. One source of these is our continued inability to apply equally acceptable measurements to highly differing kinds of values. It is easy to present the so-called hard facts, meaning dollar figures, to justify a development. It is still difficult or impossible to present equally convincing facts on environmental costs. How can you justify the continued existence of bald eagles in economic terms comparable to the X millions of dollars to be derived from various land development proposals? It is more than probable that the world would go on and man's material existence not be greatly affected if all eagles everywhere ceased to exist. But we don't know for sure. We do know that an impoverishment of human existence would take place. How do you attach a dollar value to man's intellectual, spiritual, or aesthetic welfare? The answer is that you do not. The decision whether to keep eagles or not keep eagles is ultimately a

You can compromise at Marco Island or Rookery Bay, but somewhere you must make a stand.

political decision and is not one where economic arguments are final determinants.

Not all environmental questions are as subject to debate as those involving the survival of eagles, condors, or pelicans. Where man's existence is clearly endangered or his material well-being affected, such as by the effects of a continued build-up of various environmental poisons or the destruction of the basis for support of agriculture or fisheries, we usually decide not to allow this activity to continue. But there is still room to argue, with our present deficiencies in knowledge, about how much we can poison or destroy and still continue to survive or how far we can push natural ecosystems in our pursuit of short-term gains before we make earth untenable for man. We can still argue, but one would hope that we will proceed beyond such arguments—that we will ask not how little we must have in order to survive, but how much we can have to fully appreciate life on this planet.

So long as decisions are to be made in the political arena, and it is likely that the most important ones will continue to be, it is essential that those who favor the continued existence of eagles organize for political effectiveness. Those who believe that a rich and diverse natural environment is essential for the maintenance of man's most valuable human qualities must develop political clout. Otherwise, no agency, no system of organization, will function as it was intended, and environmental review boards may serve only to rubber stamp decisions made by exploiters of the environment. Fortunately, Florida has a remarkable array of people and organizations concerned with environmental protection.

The Collier County Conservancy has been an outstanding example of an effective local organization. Over a period of several years, it has raised nearly one million dollars to buy land for conservation purposes. However, it has not operated alone. National organizations, such as the Nature Conservancy, the Audubon Society, and the Conservation Foundation, have contributed in various ways to its projects, and behind these have been still larger private foundations, such as Ford and that of the Rockefeller brothers. Nevertheless, the drive and initiative and most of the money raised have been essentially of local origin and represent evidence of the degree to which citizen support can be enlisted for protection of environmental values.

One can list many local and state organizations that have been effective in the conservation area. The Sanibel–Captiva Conservation Foundation has done a remarkable job. Far to the north, in Gainesville, the Florida Defenders of the Environment has gained an unusually broad following through concentration on the single objective of stopping the Cross-Florida Barge Canal. The Florida Audubon Society has purchased land for sanctuaries throughout Florida and has extended its efforts to include environmental protection in Latin America. Although much of the credit for halting construction of the Florida jetport must go to Walter Hickel and Russell Train for their leadership of the Department of the Interior, they could not have succeeded without the active support of virtually every national and state conservation organization.

There is no doubt that it is far easier to raise local support for preserving the local swamp than it is to muster the continuous support needed to maintain vigilance over the total Florida environment. Nevertheless, an impressive start was made in 1969, largely through the leadership of Lyman Rogers, with the formation of a political-action group known as Conservation 70s. This group has hired a full-time lobbyist to work in Tallahassee—Loring Lovell, who had learned his way around while working for the secretary of state. Conservation 70s formulated a package of conservation bills which, in their entirety, would do much to improve conditions in Florida. During the 1970 legislative session, Conservation 70s drew on its membership to provide expert witnesses at all appropriate legislative hearings. Virtually every conservation organization in Florida was involved in this effort.

There is still a need, however, to weld together the various citizens' organizations concerned with conservation into a more effective whole and to provide to each of them the information and expertise needed to function most

In 1970, wilderness, or even wild country, is in short supply. Where do you go when all the fair places have been ruined? Where do you go from Florida?

effectively. A start toward this was made in 1968 with the establishment of the Florida Conservation Foundation, but this must be broadened, strengthened, funded, and activated. Most particularly, this foundation must involve those groups not normally labeled as conservationists in order to develop the broadest base of public support.

There is no doubt that a public concern for the environment had grown enormously in Florida even before it became a major force nationally. Its growth was reflected in the editorial tone and extent of coverage in the Florida news media. Florida's legislators and administrators were at first slow to realize that the winds had changed and in consequence were caught out by storms of public protest on several occasions. It would be naïve to assume, however, that there is not rough going ahead. Developers have become more skillful at disguising their intentions in language that seems ecologically impeccable. Nevertheless, there is a willingness to work together among the conservation groups that has not been present in the past. This is hopeful, but there will remain occasions where head-on collisions are unavoidable.

It is possible to negotiate and compromise, to bargain and dicker, while all options remain open. But in time they begin to close, and the space for maneuver grows cramped. It is possible at Marco Island and Rookery Bay to seek the best compromise between conservation and development. There are other places where this still can be done. But elsewhere the time has come when it is necessary to win, once and for all, or forever lose. In Florida, generally, there has been too much retreat.

If you can't win the fight for the Florida environment, what can you win, and is it worth winning? Are you really prepared to acquiesce while the dredge-and-fill, the high-rise and low-rise developments, the highways and the jetports, the barge canals and industrial parks, cut the land to ribbons? Are you willing to wait until the pesticides accumulate and the wildlife has gone? While the waters of every stream and lake and bay become choked and filthy? Will you be willing to steer your little boat down a dirty canal into a fishless ocean? Do you really want to make extra money at the expense of your home country, knowing it can buy you only a little more of what you already have in surfeit, knowing it can buy you no refuge? Where do you go when all the fair places have been ruined? Where do you go from Florida?

References

Alexander, Taylor R. 1958. High hammock vegetation of the southern Florida mainland. *Quart. Jour. Fla. Academy of Sciences* 21 (4): 293–298.

Allen, Robert Porter. 1961. *Birds of the Caribbean.* New York: Viking.

Allen, Ross. 1969. Why save the alligator? Ocala: Conservation 70s. Mimeographed.

Allen, Ross, and Neill, W. T. 1952. The Florida crocodile. *Florida Wildlife* reprint.

Allyn, Rube. 1969. *Florida fishes.* St. Petersburg: Great Outdoors Publ. Co.

Andrews, Allen H. 1950. *A Yank pioneer in Florida.* Jacksonville: Douglas Printing Co.

Barbour, Thomas. 1944. *That vanishing Eden: A naturalist's Florida.* Boston: Little, Brown.

Barrett, Mary F. 1956. *Common exotic trees of south Florida (dicotyledons).* Gainesville: Univ. of Fla. Press.

Beck, Carol. 1969. Natural history of the Suwannee. *Florida Gardener.* Jan.–Feb. pp. 6–7.

Belue, Frank. 1969. The black wolf of Florida. *Florida Naturalist* 42 (4): 147.

Bickel, Karl A. 1942. *The mangrove coast.* New York: Coward–McCann.

Bond, James. 1961. *Birds of the West Indies.* Boston: Houghton Mifflin.

Borrelli, Pete. 1970. Eco-alert on the Cross-Florida Barge Canal. New York: Sierra Club.

Brookfield, Charles M., and Griswold, Oliver. 1949. *They all called it tropical.* (2d ed., 1964). Miami: Data Press.

Bureau of Sport Fisheries and Wildlife.

    1963. *A fish and wildlife report on Cross-Florida barge canal intracoastal waterway, Florida.* Washington, D.C.: Dept. of Interior.

    1965. *Refuges of the Florida Keys.* Washington, D.C.: Dept. of Interior.

    1967. *Birds of the Florida Keys National Wildlife Refuges.* Washington, D.C.: Dept. of Interior.

    1967. *J. N. "Ding" Darling National Wildlife Refuge.* Washington, D.C.: Dept. of Interior.

Burgess, J. Edward. 1969. *Future of Florida's fresh water resources.* Ocala: Conservation 70s. Mimeographed.

Bush, Monroe. 1968. People-pressure: A demographic look at Florida's environment. Mimeographed.

Cahn, Robert. 1969. Battle rages over Everglades park. *Christian Science Monitor.* June 14.

Carr, Archie. 1967. *So excellent a fishe: A natural history of sea turtles.* New York: Natural History Press.

Carr, Archie, and Goin, Coleman J. 1955. *Guide to the reptiles, amphibians, and fresh-water fishes of Florida.* Gainesville: Univ. of Fla. Press.

Carr, Marjorie Harris. 1965. The Oklawaha River Wilderness. *Florida Naturalist* 38 (3–A): 1–3.

Clark, John. 1967. *Fish and man: Conflict in the Atlantic estuaries.* Spec. publ. 5. Highlands, N.J.: Amer. Littoral Society.

Clement, Roland C. 1969. Marshes, developers, and taxes: A new ethic for our estuaries. *Audubon* 71 (6): 34–35.

Cloudy sunshine state. 1970. *Time.* Apr. 13. pp. 48–49.

Conservation Foundation. 1968. *Rookery Bay Area Project.* Washington, D.C.

Craighead, Frank C., Sr. 1963. *Orchids and other air plants of the Everglades National Park.* Coral Gables: Univ. of Miami Press.

————. 1968. The role of the alligator in shaping plant communities and maintaining wildlife in the southern Everglades. *Florida Naturalist* 41 (1, 2).

————. 1969. Some biological aspects of the water situation

in the Everglades National Park and vicinity. Xerox report.

―――. 1970. Two mysteries of the Everglades. *Florida Naturalist* 43 (2): 51–52.

―――. 1969. Vegetation and recent sedimentation in Everglades National Park. *Florida Naturalist* 42 (4): 157–166.

Cruickshank, Helen G. 1948. *Flight into sunshine.* New York: Macmillan.

Darlington, P. J. 1938. The origin of the fauna of the Greater Antilles with discussion of dispersal of animals over water and through the air. *Quarterly Review of Biology* 13 (3): 274–300.

Dasmann, Raymond F. 1965. *The Destruction of California.* New York: Macmillan.

―――. 1969. *National parks and the problems of our environment.* Washington, D.C.: Conservation Foundation.

Dasmann, Raymond F.; Carr, M. H.; Partington, W. M.; Robertson, W. B. eds. 1970. *Environmental impact of the Cross-Florida Barge Canal with special emphasis on the Oklawaha Regional Ecosystem.* Gainesville: Florida Defenders of the Environment.

Davis, J. H., Jr. 1943. *The natural features of southern Florida.* Fla. Geological Survey Bull. 25: 5–311.

Dickey, R. D.; West, Erdman; and Mowhy, Harold. 1966. *Native and exotic palms of Florida.* Agric. Extension Service Bull. 152–A. Gainesville: Univ. of Fla. Press.

Douglas, Marjorie Stoneman. 1947. *The Everglades: River of grass.* Coconut Grove: Hurricane House.

Elton, Charles. 1959. *The ecology of invasions by animals and plants.* London: Methuen.

Ehrenfeld, David W. 1970. *Biological conservation.* New York: Holt, Rinehart and Winston.

Espenshade, Edward B., Jr. 1960. *Goode's world atlas.* Chicago: Rand McNally.

Farb, Peter. 1965. Disaster threatens the Everglades. *Audubon* 67 (5): 302–309.

Federal Water Pollution Control Administration. 1968. *Clean water for the nation's estuaries.* 3 vols. Washington, D.C.: Dept. of Interior.

Federal Writers' Project. 1939. *Florida: A guide to the southernmost state.* New York: Oxford.

Finch, Vernon, and Trewartha, G. T. 1942. *Elements of geography, physical and cultural.* New York: McGraw-Hill.

Fisher, James; Simon, Noel; and Vincent, Jack. 1969. *Wildlife in danger.* New York: Viking Press.

Florida Forest Service. 1969. Florida's Torreya tree. *Florida Naturalist* 42 (1): 11–12.

Fritz, Florence. 1963. *Unknown Florida.* Coral Gables: Univ. of Miami Press.

Frye, O. Earl, Jr. 1970. *A brief assessment of the ecological impact of the Cross-Florida Barge Canal.* Florida Game and Fresh-water Fish Commission. Mimeographed report.

Funk, Ben, and Murray, Frank. 1969. Born of emotion, canal still in furor. Jacksonville: *Times-Union & Journal.* Dec. 21.

Gill, A. M., and Tomlinson, P. B. 1969. Studies of the growth of the red mangrove (*Rhizophora mangle* L.). *Biotropica* 1 (1): 1–9.

Glooschenko, Valerie. 1969. Cross roads for Everglades National Park. *Florida Naturalist* 42 (4–B).

Glooschenko, W. A., and Glooschenko, V. A. 1969. Thermal pollution. *Florida Naturalist* 42 (1): 3–7.

Goldberger, Marvin, and MacDonald, Gordon J. F. 1970. *Environmental problems in South Florida.* Washington, D.C.: National Academy of Sciences.

Golley, Frank; Odum, H. T.; and Wilson, R. F. 1962. The structure and metabolism of a Puerto Rican red mangrove forest in May. *Ecology* 43: 9–18.

Governor's Aquatic Research and Development Committee. 1968. Report. Ocala. Mimeographed.

Griswold, Oliver. 1965. *The Florida Keys and the coral reef.* Miami: Graywood Press.

Hargreaves, Dorothy, and Hargreaves, Bob. 1960. *Tropical blossoms.* Portland, Ore.: Hargreaves Industrial.

————. 1964. *Tropical trees.* Portland, Ore.: Hargreaves Industrial.

Harlow, Richard, and Jones, F. K., Jr. 1965. *The white-tailed deer in Florida.* Florida Game and Fresh-water Fish Commission Tech. Bull. 9.

Harlow, William H., and Harrar. E. S. 1941. *Textbook of dendrology.* New York: McGraw-Hill.

Harper, Francis, ed. 1958. *The travels of William Bartram.* Naturalist's edition. New Haven: Yale.

Harrar, Ellwood S., and Harrar, J. George. 1962. *Guide to southern trees.* New York: Dover.

Harris, Robert C. 1970. *The endangered Everglades.* Mimeographed report.

Hartman, Daniel S. 1969. Florida's manatees: Mermaids in peril. *National Geographic* 136 (3): 342–353.

Heald, Eric J. 1969. *The production of organic detritus in a south Florida estuary.* Dissertation. Coral Gables: Univ. of Miami.

Herald, Earl S. 1961. *Living fishes of the world.* Rev. ed., 1962. New York: Doubleday.

Hines, T. C.; Fogarty, M. J.; and Chappell, L. C. 1968. Alligator research in Florida. 22d annual conf. Southeast Assoc. Game and Fish Commissioners. Mimeographed.

Holdridge, L. R. 1947. Determination of world plant formations from simple climatic data. *Science* 105: 367–368.

Hutt, Arthur P. 1967. The American alligator. *National Parks* 41 (2–3): 14–17.

Idyll, C. P.; Tabb, D. C.; and Yokel, B. 1967. Conservation in Biscayne Bay. *Florida Naturalist* 40 (3): 77–81.

Idyll, C. P. 1969. New Florida resident: The walking catfish. *National Georgraphic* 135 (6): 846.

Jehl, Joseph R., Jr. 1970. A wonderful bird was the pelican. *Oceans* 1: 11–19.

Kahl, M. Phillip, Jr. 1964. Food ecology of the wood stork in Florida. *Ecological Monographs* 34 (2): 97–117.

King, Wayne. 1968. As a consequence many will die. *Florida Naturalist* 41 (3): 99–103, 120.

Kolipinski, M. C., and Higer, A. L. 1966. Ecological research in Everglades National Park. *National Parks* 40: 14–17.

Komarek, E. V. ed. 1965. *Proceedings: 4th annual Tall Timbers Fire Ecology Conf.*, Tallahassee.

————. 1969. *Proceedings: Tall Timbers Conf. on ecological animal control by habitat management.* Tallahassee.

Koopman, Karl F. 1959. The zoogeographical limits of the West Indies. *Journal Mammalogy* 40 (2): 236–240.

Krakauer, Thomas. 1970. The invasion of the toads. *Florida Naturalist* 43 (1): 12–14.

Kuchler, A. W. 1964. *Potential natural vegetation of the conterminous United States.* Special publ. 36. Map and Manual. American Geographical Society.

Kuperberg, Joel. 1969. Acquisition by plan. 20th Annual Conf., Nature Conservancy. Mimeographed.

Kurz, Herman, and Godfrey, R. K. 1962. *Trees of northern Florida.* Gainesville: Univ. of Fla. Press.

Larson, Robert W. 1952. *The timber supply situation in Florida.* Forest Service, Research Report 6, Washington, D.C.: Dept. of Agriculture.

Lauff, George H., ed. 1967. *Estuaries.* Washington, D.C.: American Assoc. Advancement of Science Publ. 83.

Laycock, George. 1969. Where have all the pelicans gone? *Audubon* 71 (5): 10–17.

LeBuff, Charles R., Jr. 1969. *The marine turtles of Sanibel and Captiva Islands, Florida.* Spec. publ. 1. Sanibel–Captiva Conservation Foundation.

Legislator's environmental guide. 1969. Ocala: Conservation 70s.

Leopold, Luna B. 1969. *Environmental impact of the Everglades jetport.* Washington, D.C.: Dept. of Interior.

Levine, Paul. 1970. Beware of golden voices and swampy land. *St. Petersburg Times.* March 15.

Little, Elbert L., Jr., and Wadsworth, F. H. 1964. *Common trees of Puerto Rico and the Virgin Islands.* Washington, D.C.: United States Government Printing Office.

Lyons, Ernest. 1969. *My Florida.* New York: A. S. Barnes.

MacDonald, John D. 1962. *A flash of green.* Greenwich, Conn.: Fawcett Gold Medal.

————. 1968. The Florida Keys in Hurricane Alley. *Holiday.* December.

Marshall, Arthur R. 1969. Population and the Florida environment. Ocala: Conservation 70s. Mimeographed.

Maxwell, Lewis S. 1959. *Florida insects: Their habits and control.* Tampa: Lewis Maxwell.

Matthiessen, Peter. 1970. The river-eater. *Audubon* 72 (2): 52–53.

McCoy, H. J. 1962. *Ground-water resources of Collier County, Florida.* Tallahassee: Fla. Geological Survey Report 31.

McLane, William M. 1969. *The aquatic plant business in relation to infestations of exotic aquatic plants in Florida waters.* Mimeographed report.

McQuigg, John L. 1965. The economic value of preserving the natural shoreline. Stuart, Fla.: Univ. Fla. Bulkhead Seminar. Mimeographed.

Menke, Charlotte R. 1968. *Economic study of the Biscayne National Monument.* Gainesville: Univ. of Fla. Press.

Miller, James N. 1970. *Rape on the Oklawaha.* Reprint. Pleasantville, N.Y.: *Reader's Digest.*

Miller, Julie. 1969. The Sanibel. *Florida Naturalist* 42: 126–7, 142.

Milton, John, and Farvar, M. Taghi. 1970. *The careless technology.* New York: Natural History Press.

Morgan, Tom. 1969. Conservancy obtains right to 10,000 isles. *Miami Herald.* Dec. 12.

Mowry, H.; Toy, L. R.; and Wolve, H. S. 1967. *Miscellaneous tropical and subtropical Florida fruits.* Agric. Extension Serv. Bull. 156. Gainesville: Univ. of Fla. Press.

Murphy, Robert. 1968. *Wild sanctuaries.* New York: E. P. Dutton.

National Park Service. 1967. *Biscayne National Monument: A proposal.* Washington, D. C.: Dept. of Interior.

————. 1968. *Proceedings of the 2d meeting on natural sciences research conducted in Everglades National Park and the South Florida region.* Washington, D.C.: Dept. of Interior.

Newsom, John D., ed. 1968. *Proceedings of the Marsh and*

Estuary Management Symposium. Baton Rouge: Louisiana State University.

Olsen, S. J. 1959. *Fossil mammals of Florida.* Tallahassee: Fla. Geological Survey Spec. Publ. 6.

Outdoor Recreation Resources Review Commission. 1962. *Outdoor recreation for America.* Washington, D.C.: ORRRC.

Padrick, Robert W. 1968. Wilderness in Florida: Heritage and challenge. Mimeographed.

———. 1968. *Recreation in the Everglades.* Unnumbered pamphlet. West Palm Beach: Central & Southern Florida Flood Control District.

Parker, Garald G., and Cooke, C. Wythe. 1944. *Late Cenozoic geology of southern Florida with a discussion of the ground water.* Tallahassee: Fla. Geological Survey Bull. 27.

Partington, William M. 1967. The Everglades: Ecological puzzle. *Animal Kingdom* 70 (5): 135–141.

———. 1969. Oklawaha: The fight is on again. *Living Wilderness.* Autumn. pp. 19–23.

Plager, Sheldon J., and Maloney, F. E. 1968. *Controlling waterfront development.* Studies in Public Administration 30. Gainesville: Univ. of Fla. Press.

Pothier, Dick. 1968. Animal imports too risky? *Miami Herald.* July 14.

Provost, Maurice W. 1968. *Sanibel Island: Geology, topography, vegetation.* Mimeographed.

———. 1969. Man, mosquitoes, and birds. *Florida Naturalist* reprint.

———. 1969. The pesticide menace to a healthful environment. Ocala: Conservation 70s. Mimeographed.

A quarter century of progress. 1943–1968. 1968. Tallahassee: Florida Game and Fresh-water Fish Commission.

Raftery, John C. 1969. Everglades National Park: The Future. 33d annual meeting, Fla. Academy of Science, Gainesville. Mimeographed.

———. 1969. Adverse environmental influences on the Everglades. Mimeographed.

Raisz, Erwin, and associates. 1964. *Atlas of Florida*. Gainesville: Univ. of Fla. Press.

Reid, George K. 1969. Overview of destructive forces in the present and future of Florida's fresh water. Mimeographed.

Reybold, E. 1942. *Waterway across northern Florida for barge traffic*. Washington, D.C.: Govt. Printing Office.

Richards, P. W. 1952. *The tropical rain forest*. Cambridge: Cambridge Univ. Press.

Risebrough, R. W.; Rieche, P.; Peakall, D. B.; Herman, S. G.; and Kirvey, M. N. 1968. Polychlorinated biphenyls in the global ecosystem. *Nature* 220 (5172): 1098–1101.

Robertson, William B., Jr. 1959. *Everglades: The park story*. Coral Gables: Univ. of Miami Press.

——. 1970. Transatlantic migration of sooty terns. *Florida Naturalist* 43 (1): 15–18.

Rosenberg, W. P. 1968. *Damage report of the road-clearing project through Elliott Key Park*. Dade Co. Park and Recreation Dept. Report.

Schell, Rolfe. 1962. *1,000 years on Mound Key*. Fort Meyers Beach, Fla.: Island Press.

Scholl, D. W.; Craighead, F. C.; and Stuiver, M. 1968. Florida submergence curve revised: Its relation to coastal sedimentation rates. *Science* 163: 562–564.

Seaman, Elwood A. 1969. *Guidelines for the future of controlling exotic fishes*. Mimeographed.

Sea slicks: a reservoir for pesticides. *26° N 80° W*. 1970. 1 (2): 1. Coral Gables: Univ. of Miami.

Shantz, H. L., and Zon, R. 1924. *Atlas of American agriculture*. Washington, D.C.: Dept. of Agriculture.

Shelford, Victor E. 1963. *The ecology of North America*. Urbana: Univ. of Illinois.

Siekman, Lula. Undated. *Handbook of Florida shells*. St. Petersburg: Great Outdoors Publishing Co.

Simon, Marion. 1968. We were going to get it all for $59.95 each. *National Observer*. Dec. 2.

Sims, Harold. 1969. Boca Ciega Bay Story. *Florida Naturalist* 42 (3-A): 2–3.

Skala, Martin. 1968. Free-wheeling land sales fade. *Christian Science Monitor*. Oct. 5.

Small, John K. 1929. *From Eden to Sahara: Florida's tragedy.* Science Press, privately printed.

Smith, A. W. 1967. Water for Everglades National Park. *National Parks* 41 (243): 2.

Smith, F. B., *et al.* 1967. *Principal soil areas of Florida.* Agric. Experiment Station Bull. 717. Gainesville: Univ. of Fla. Press.

Southern biologists worried by walking catfish threat. 1969. *South Carolina Wildlife* 16 (4): 4, 15.

Sprunt, Alexander, Jr. 1954. *Florida bird life.* With Addendum, 1963. New York: Coward–McCann and National Audubon Society.

Stephens, William M. 1968. *Southern seashores.* New York: Holiday House.

Straight, Michael. 1965. The water picture in Everglades National Park. *National Parks* 39 (215): 4–9.

Taylor, Robert L. 1961. *A journey to Matecumbe.* New York: Signet, New American Library.

Teal, John, and Teal, Mildred. 1969. *Life and death of a salt marsh.* Boston: Atlantic Monthly Press.

Tebeau, Charlton W. 1957. *Florida's last frontier: The history of Collier County.* Coral Gables: Univ. of Miami Press.

———. 1963. *They lived in the park.* Coral Gables: Univ. of Miami Press.

Torrey, Bradford. 1924. *A Florida sketch-book.* Boston: Houghton Mifflin.

True, David O., ed. 1945. Memoir of D°. d'Escalante Fontaneda respecting Florida. Written in Spain about the year 1575. Translated from the Spanish with notes by Buckingham Smith, Washington, D.C., 1854.

Udall, Stewart L. 1963. *The quiet crisis.* New York: Holt, Rinehart and Winston.

———. 1969. *Beyond the impasse: The Dade jetport and the environment of south Florida.* Washington, D.C.: *Overview.*

United States Army Corps of Engineers. 1969. *Cross-Florida Barge Canal.* Folder. Jacksonville.

Vines, William. 1967. Florida beach resources management needs. *Florida Planning and Development* 18 (6): 1, 4–8. Boca Raton: Fla. Atlantic Univ.

———. 1969. *Palm Beach County recreation and open space.* 2 vols. West Palm Beach: Area planning board of Palm Beach County.

Voss, Gilbert L., *et al.* 1969. *Report of the committee on inshore and estuarine pollution.* New York: Hoover Foundation.

Waldron, Martin. 1969. Walking catfish spread over a thousand square-mile area in Florida. *New York Times.* July 6.

Weaver, John E., and Clements, F. E. 1938. *Plant ecology.* New York: McGraw-Hill.

Welsh, Charles A. 1959. *The economic prospects of Cross-Florida barge canal project.* Winter Park: Rollins College Press.

West, Erdman, and Arnold, L. E. 1956. *The native trees of Florida.* Gainesville: Univ. of Fla. Press.

White, Louise V., and Smiley, Nora K. 1959. *History of Key West.* St. Petersburg: Great Outdoors Publishing Co.

Whitney, Elizabeth. 1970. The swamp peddlers. *St. Petersburg Times.* May 3–8.

Wilson, Edward O., and Eisner, Thomas. 1969. Lignum Vitae: Relict island. *Natural History.*

Woodburn, Kenneth D. 1969. Submerged land management for Florida. Mimeographed.

Wright, C. E. 1969. The pelican finds a haven in Florida. *New York Times.* Nov. 30.

Wurster, Charles F. 1969. DDT stands trial. *Audubon* 71 (5): 128–136.

Zahl, Paul A. 1969. The magic lure of sea-shells. *National Geographic* 135 (3): 386–429.

Zim, Herbert S. 1960. *A guide to Everglades National Park and the nearby Florida Keys.* New York: Golden Press.

Index

Index

236

Index

Index

Ponce de León, Juan, 46, 104, 130
Population: ecological environment and, 179–204; growth of, 6; makeup, 52–56
Porter, Commodore, 143
Pothier, Dick, 158
Power plant, atomic, 120–21
Preserves, 127–35
Private agencies, land control and, 200–201
Provost, Maurice, 139–40
Puma, 35

Raccoons, 90
Railroads, Florida Keys, 106–107
Raleigh, Sir Walter, 48
Randall Act (1967), 69
Rattlesnakes, 11, 42
Real estate entrepeneurs: Rookery Bay and, 59–79
Red-breasted merganser ducks, 138
Red mangrove, 65–68
Red-whiskered bulbul, 175–76
Reddish egrets, 44, 138
Redhead ducks, 138
Reed, Nathaniel P., 127–28
Refuges: Everglades National Park, 41, 72–74, 80–96, 99, 112–13; Great White Heron, 114–15, 124; Key Deer, 115–17, 118, 124; Key West National Wildlife, 113–114; Rookery Bay, 57–79
Regional development, wildlife and, 59
Reid, George, 164
Remuda Ranch Grants, 195
Reptiles, 27, 39–42; Age of, 25
Republican Party, 52
Review boards, environmental, 211–12
Rhizophora mangle, 65
Rhizophoraceae, 65
Rhodes Key, 118
Ridley turtles, 41

Ring-necked ducks, 138
Roads, maintenance of, 188–90
Robertson, Bill, 89
Robertson, Dr. William, 74
Rodman Pool, 162
Rogers, Lyman, 156, 219
Rookery Bay, 210, 221; struggle over, 57–79
Roosevelt Channel, 136
Roosevelt, Theodore, 141
Roseate spoonbills, 44, 92, 102, 111, 138; protection of, 112
Ross Allen's Reptile Institute (Silver Springs), 40
Russia, 207–208

Sailfish, 42
Sailors, Spanish, 104
St. Lucie Canal, 129, 145
St. Vincent's Island, ecology of, 131–35
Sambar deer, 135
San Carlos Bay, 135
Sanctuary, Rookery Bay, 62–79. *See also* Refuges
Sand hickory tree, 32
Sand pine trees, 34, 132
Sanford, Nelson, 63
Sanibel-Captiva Conservation Foundation, 142, 218
Sanibel-Captiva Islands, 135–42, 167; birds of, 138–39; and mosquitos, 139–40
Sanibel Light, 139
Satterthwaite, Ann, 74
Saw palmetto trees, 34
Scaled pigeon, 103
Scarlet ibis, 176
Schinus terebinthifolius, 167
School of Atmospheric and Marine Sciences, 73
Scissor-tailed flycatcher, 103
Scrub oak tree, 34
Scuba diving, 117

242

Index

United Nations, 214
UNESCO, 214
University of Florida, 107
University of Miami, 62, 67, 72, 73, 108, 165

Vegetation, 27, 29–34; climate and, 12–15; of Florida Keys, 108–10; pests, 158–71; of St. Vincent's Island, 132–34. *See also* individual names
Vero Beach, 139
Vertebrate fossils, 24–26
Vines, Bill, 72, 73, 74
Virginia white-tailed deer, 37
Volpe, John, 94–95
Vultures, 28

Wace, Nigel, 172, 174
Wallace, George, 52
Water hyacinth, 134; problem of, 158–62
Water oak trees, 32
Water pollution, 2, 157–67; weeds and, 158–64
Water system, Everglades National Park, 87–93
Waterfront development, 191
Waterways, 143–54
Watson, Jack, 114, 116
Weather, 9–21

Wetlands, canal and, 144–49
Whelks, 137
White herons, 92, 103
White ibises, 44
Water lilies, 134
Weeds, pest, 161–64
White-tailed deer, 134
Widgeon ducks, 137–38
Wild hogs, 135
Wild life, 27–44; sanctuaries, 62–79, 80–96, 99, 112–26
Wildlife Management Institute, 116
Wilson, Edward, 122
White-crowned pigeons, 122
White mangrove, 65–66
Wolves, 28
Wood storks, 88, 92–93, 132, 138
World War II, 68, 89, 110, 131, 140, 147
Wreckers, 104–106

Yellow-crowned night heron, 138
Yokel, Bernie, 73

Zamia plant, 108
Zebras, 135
Zenaida dove, 103
Zones, Life, 13
Zoning, land, 193–94